It's Your Money!

isn't it?

It's Your Money!

isn't it?

G. EDWARD REID

REVIEW AND HERALD® PUBLISHING ASSOCIATION
HAGERSTOWN, MD 21740

Copyright ©1993 by
Review and Herald® Publishing Association

The author assumes full responsibility for the accuracy of all facts and quotations as cited in this book.

Unless otherwise noted, Bible texts in this book are from The New King James Version. Copyright © 1979, 1980, 1982, Thomas Nelson, Inc., Publishers.

Texts credited to NIV are from the *Holy Bible, New International Version.* Copyright © 1973, 1978, 1984, International Bible Society. Used by permission of Zondervan Bible Publishers.

Verses marked TLB are taken from *The Living Bible,* copyright© 1971 by Tyndale House Publishers, Wheaton, Ill. Used by permission.

This book was
Edited by Gerald Wheeler
Designed by Bill Kirstein
Cover art by Patricia Wegh
Typeset: 11/13 Times Roman

PRINTED IN U.S.A.

98 97 96 95 94 93   10 9 8 7 6 5 4 3 2

R&H Cataloging Service
Reid, G. Edward
   It's your money! (isn't it?)

   1. Personal finance. I. Title.
   332.024

ISBN 0-8280-0726-8

Revised Edition

Dedication

To my dear wife, Kathy, who has shared my life, managed our personal finances, and learned and practiced with me the biblical principles of money management.

CONTENTS

Foreword

What you are about to discover in this book will be new to many readers—very new! To some the principles will seem radical. They will even appear foolish to a non-Christian.

I have written this book for those who have accepted Jesus Christ as their Saviour and are seeking to make Him Lord of their lives as well.

The materialistically oriented cannot fathom that it really is more blessed to give than to receive, and that life does not consist in the abundance of our possessions. This book will illustrate the importance of these principles.

My book takes the reader several steps beyond traditional stewardship, especially in the areas of tithing, home purchase and ownership, debt elimination, retirement income, investments, and estate planning. The reader will also notice a sense of urgency in this book regarding money management in the light of the fast-fulfilling signs of the second coming of our Lord and Saviour.

"Do not love the world or the things in the world. If anyone loves the world, the love of the Father is not in him.

"For all that is in the world—the lust of the flesh, the lust of the eyes, and the pride of life—is not of the Father but is of the world.

"And the world is passing away, and the lust of it; but he who does the will of God abides forever" (1 John 2:15-17).

Love Not the World

World economic conditions have nearly everyone concerned. The anxiety level is at an all-time high as the jet set has become the debt set. The majority of the world lives in abject poverty, and even the most affluent nations have been struggling with a terrible recession. In the United States just the interest on the debt load itself has begun to crush us. Many economists predict that before the year 2000 it will take all the revenues generated by the tax system just to pay the interest on the national debt.

Where does this situation leave your family and mine? Families are breaking up at an alarming rate, and most point to financial difficulties as a major factor. Business and personal bankruptcies escalate year after year. In 1989 the United States alone had 12,365 personal (family) bankruptcies *every week* according to the *Wall Street Journal* of February 21, 1990. The next year the number rose to 14,600 families per week, and 1991 saw an average of 17,300 family bankruptcies each and every week. The 1992 rate reached more than 20,000 per week.

Personal Bankruptcies

This growing list of personal bankruptcies has a rippling effect on the entire economy. Because of thousands of real estate mortgage defaults, banks are failing at record rates. Businesses must consolidate or die, and even major corporations are experiencing setbacks, plant closures, unheard-of losses, and thousands being laid off. Perhaps the magnitude of our financial problems today can be underscored by the announcement by former New Hampshire Republican senator Warren Rudman that he would not seek a third term. Easily reelectable, Rudman, along with colleague Phil Gramm, tried to seek fiscal responsibility with the Gramm-Rudman initiative to balance the federal budget. Rudman stated as his reason for leaving the U.S. Senate: "The problem is the various special-interest groups. . . . It is very hard to get anything done here. . . . We are literally ignoring our single most pressing problem—the deficit—which is going to destroy the country and cause the financial markets at some point to collapse, the currency to be devalued; all that people have saved will be worthless unless we do something about it.

"We are reaching the thin edge, and every economist knows it. You're talking a national debt that will equal the annual GNP by 1999" (*U.S. News & World Report*, Apr. 6, 1992, p. 19).

The state of the economy played a major role in the 1992 presidential election. No president in recent history had a higher approval rating (over 90 percent) than George Bush just one year before the election. However, when the dust settled and the election results were in, Bill Clinton had defeated Bush. Why? Exit polls revealed that in spite of all the rhetoric about abortion and family values during the campaign, only 12 percent of the voters had these factors on their minds when they cast their votes, but an amazing 68 percent considered the economy and its problems as the main factor in determining their choice.

Even before the inauguration, however, President-elect Clinton emphasized that things were worse than he had believed, and that the American public should not expect any miracles. He stated that he planned to assemble a large group of financial experts to study the situation and made recommendations. In effect he was saying, "We really don't know exactly what to do, but we will try one thing, and if that doesn't work, we'll do something else, hoping that we will at last find whatever will make a difference."

American Dream Now a Nightmare

For many the American dream has become a nightmare. Definitions of the American dream vary somewhat, but the basic concept in the minds of many people has centered on financial success or secular accomplishments. Early in our history most would have defined the American dream as a nice home, a happy family, a good education, a stable job, and the chance to excel, to get ahead.

Today American advertising and education have taught people to become selfish, worldly, and materialistic. A few months ago while driving north of Atlanta on I-75 I noticed in my rearview mirror that a large motor home was overtaking me. It was a Bluebird Wanderlodge, top-of-the-line edition. Visible extras included chrome wheels, retractable satellite dish, etc. The motor home was towing a tandem-axle trailer that was hauling his and her motorcycles riding sideways across the front of the trailer. The bulk of the trailer carried an Acura Legend coupe. As this outfit passed me I noted on the back bumper of the trailer the now well-known slogan "He who dies with the most toys wins." My immediate reaction was "This guy must be on a suicide run—he has it all with him now!"

Other popular slogans express similar sentiments: "Excess is the American way." "You owe it to yourself." "Pay yourself first." "Look out for number one." Unfortunately, these are not just trite expressions. Many believe and practice them.

Our work ethic has deteriorated to the point that most employers will pay their employees just enough to keep them from quitting, and most employees work just hard enough to keep from getting fired. Those working have a tendency to think about two things: payday (the weekend) and retirement (when they can get out of the rat race).

Our capitalistic society emphasizes ownership and the accumulation of possessions. We have built an affluent society based upon a sand foundation of future debt. All that we have is in danger of being wiped out by any financial crisis, even a relatively minor one. But this need not apply to those who understand and obey God's financial principles. His financial wisdom builds to last, not to impress others.

What concerns me as a Christian professional is that the attitudes and conditions that I have described above are diametrically opposed to biblical principles of finance and money management. It is even more serious when we realize that most "Christian" families have followed the example of the world in money management. God's plan for us is that we are to be the salt of the earth. However, in many cases the world is salting us!

In the Old Testament Samson had to travel to the camp of the Philistines. When Samson became involved with Delilah, she was not the girl next door. He had to walk a great distance to visit her. Conditions are very different now. When I ask in my seminars, "Where is the camp of the Philistines today?" the typical responses include "We are living right in the middle of the camp of the Philistines" or "It's in our own living rooms."

Following the World Financially

As a result, Christians who claim to take the Bible as their rule of faith and practice find themselves following the world in financial and other matters. For example, if a non-Christian decides to buy a new home and needs to borrow a portion of the money to make the purchase, he or she goes to the bank and gets a loan for 30 years. The next in line for a home loan is a Christian, and what does that person do? Anything different? Unfortunately not! In most cases the Christian will also go for the 30-year mortgage in spite of the fact that the Bible indicates that one should not be in debt longer than seven years (see Deuteronomy 15:1, etc.).

Many Christians get involved in the same financial practices as their non-Christian peers—the same get-rich-quick schemes, money-hoarding habits, credit card spending, overindulgence, heavy debt, and wrong concepts about investments, insurance, estate planning, and retirement, to name a few.

What is a Christian to do? Do we have any counsel regarding proper methods of money management? The answer is yes—very definitely yes! Through His Word, God has given specific guidelines to direct our lives so that we can enjoy the blessings that He promises us. Scripture refers more than 1,600 times to money, possessions, and humanity's attitude toward them. The New Testament discusses only love more often than it does money, which says something about the importance of money.

More than two thirds of Jesus' parables deal with money or possessions. Of particular interest to our generation is the fact that all three of the parables of Matthew 25, dealing with conditions in the church at the time of Christ's second coming, use money as a primary factor to distinguish between the saved and the lost.

Although the Bible has much to say about money and its proper management, few have taken the time to delve deeply into the subject. I thank God that He has allowed me to be placed in a position where I could learn over a period of time to value the biblical principles of personal money management. My wife, Kathy, and I have had the opportunity to study with Larry Burkett and his staff at Christian Financial Concepts for about three years. We were so impressed and blessed with what we learned that it has been a life-changing experience for us.

Following it, I examined the writings of Ellen White to determine what, if any, counsel she may have given in money management. Here again I found a wealth of excellent counsel—principles that make sense, principles that others have discovered in their search for truth.

With this great treasure of counsel, coupled with our personal testimony of its life-changing impact, we have had the privilege of conducting weekend seminars about biblical principles of personal money management in numerous churches, camp meetings, and ministerial meetings during the past few years. In addition we have had the opportunity of counseling with dozens of couples seeking financial management assistance. It is with this background and our current economic conditions that I have agreed to write this book, hoping that you will come to know those same life-changing principles.

This is not just another book about budgets, tax savings, shrewd investment strategies, get-rich-quick schemes, etc. Christian bookstores offer valuable titles by such well-known Christian authors as Larry Burkett, whom I personally highly respect and appreciate. I would recommend to the reader to examine Christian authors on this subject. Instead, this book is unique in that I have written it for a very narrow segment of society—those Christians who want to know what God's counsel is in regard to a subject that He spent a good deal of time talking about, and about which everyone must give an account.

It seeks to address Christians who accept the Bible as the authoritative Word of God, a guide for faith and practice in our present society. This book will also incorporate counsel from the writings of Ellen G. White, a person who I believe was inspired of God to speak and write on topics of vital spiritual and eschatological significance.

Financial Gurus

I consider it unfortunate that many Christians are turning to secular finance gurus such as Charles Givens (wealth without risk), who, though they share many good money management principles, have as the basic point in each strategy the goal of wealth. Many of these individuals teach how to get rich at the expense of others. They at times urge people to pay themselves first, to look out for number one, to consider that they owe it to themselves first.

As I mentioned in the preface, much of the material in this book will be new concepts to many readers. In order to understand properly the total concept of Christian money management, I would highly recommend that you read the book in the sequence I have written it. Don't just go to the chapters that you think will interest you the most. As you will note in the table of contents, I have divided the book into three sections. The first four chapters deal with the overall spiritual implications of money management and serve as the foundation for the whole book. Without this foundational material, many of the principles outlined in the following chapters will not make sense.

The middle section is the meat for which most would buy this book. It contains information both on why debt is so bad and how to get out of it. These chapters suggest how to set up a budget for your family so that you can live within your means and free up the surplus God wants you to have so that you can become more involved in helping to take the gospel to all the world. Also they discuss home ownership, with tips on ways to finance your home and save thousands of dollars compared to a conventional mortgage.

The third and final section will contain information that only those who have digested the first eight chapters will understand and practice. My prayer is that each reader will see the pieces of the financial puzzle fall into place until a clear picture emerges—a picture of successful Christian money management. May God's Spirit enlighten your mind as you read.

APPLICATION
Chapter 1

1. Read 1 Corinthians 10:31 and then determine whether or not this test would apply to money management. Why or why not?

2. Do financial problems and a materialistic society fit into the biblical end-time picture? See 2 Timothy 3:1-4 and 1 John 2:15-17.

3. Is bankruptcy an alternative for the Christian in debt? List the reasons for your answer now, and then consider the question again after reading this book.

4. Why does money management play such a vital role in the Christian experience?

◆

CHAPTER TWO

"For what will it profit a man if he gains the whole world, and loses his own soul?
"Or what will a man give in exchange for his soul?" (Mark 8:36, 37).

Eternal Life in the Balance

People never seem to have enough! From early childhood we find ourselves employing the word "mine." Somehow we feel that whatever we have or get we must hold on to for our own use. When God's river of blessing flows to us, we want to dam it up and make a recreation lake for ourselves.

In this chapter we are going to see why money is such a big deal in the life of a Christian. Evidently God knew that men and women would have a tendency to be selfish and to want to accumulate things to foster pride and provide a false sense of security. So He counseled us, "Take heed and beware of covetousness, for one's life does not consist in the abundance of the things he possesses" (Luke 12:15).

Elsewhere He said, "No servant can serve two masters. Either he will hate the one and love the other, or he will be devoted to the one and despise the other. You cannot serve both God and Money" (Luke 16:13, NIV).

It is an either/or situation. Men are either working for themselves or God. "The Pizza Man Chooses God," the story of Tom Monaghan in the *U.S. News & World Report* of July 29, 1991, illustrates this. Let me share a few excerpts from the story.

"The bottom line for Domino's owner Tom Monaghan has shifted from thin crust and deep dish to sin and salvation." Now the pizza business and almost everything Tom has is for sale. "Monaghan, 54, chose to sell so that he could devote all his time and more of his fortune, estimated at $500 million, to . . . charity.

"The ostentatious executive who was once dubbed 'the Malcolm Forbes of the Midwest' because of his lavish spending on cars, boats, planes, Detroit's major league baseball team and anything designed by Frank Lloyd Wright is now in full repentance. 'I've realized for a while I have a fault with trying to impress people,' says Monaghan. 'I justified everything I bought as an investment in the business. I wasn't just buying a car. I was making an investment and promoting Domino's, a company built on wheels. So I spent $8.1 million and bought the best car in the world [a 1931 Bugatti Royale].'

"Now each dawn brings a much bigger challenge for Monaghan, the chance to become less of a sinner and more of a saint. . . .

" 'Intellectually, the most important thing in my life is that I not go to hell . . . hell is worse than anything.'. . .

"He has sold the Sikorsky S-76 helicopter, which used to ferry him to business meetings and ball games. The eight-seat jet is gone. And the Bentley Turbo, which he never drove, the Rolls-Royce, which he never used, and the 190-foot sloop, which he never sailed, have all been unloaded. [Now he has even sold the Detroit Tigers.]

" 'My wife says I go overboard on religion,' admits Monaghan. 'But I don't know how you can.' "

The Bible speaks of "men of corrupt minds and destitute of the truth, who suppose that godliness is a means of gain. From such withdraw yourself. Now godliness with contentment is great gain. For we brought nothing into this world, and it is certain we can carry nothing out. And having food and clothing, with these we shall be content. But those who desire to be rich fall into temptation and a snare, and into many foolish and harmful lusts which drown men in destruction and perdition. For the love of money is a root of all kinds of evil, for which some have strayed from the faith in their greediness, and pierced themselves through with many sorrows. . . . Command those who are rich in this present age not to be haughty, nor to trust in uncertain riches but in the living God, who gives us richly all things to enjoy" (1 Timothy 6:5-17).

Trusting God for Everything

For some reason we human beings tend to feel that we can trust God for our eternal existence, but when it comes to this life and its needs we are on our own. But I believe that before Jesus returns the second time we will all have learned to trust Him fully, not just for our eternal life but also for the very food we eat.

As I have conducted my personal finance seminars in churches over the past few years, I have observed a strange but predictable phenomena. When people see the announcement that I will be holding a seminar on the biblical principles of personal money management on Friday night and Sabbath, discussing such topics as debt elimination, paying off your house, investments, and estate planning, a number will stay away from the program because they don't think that we should talk about money in church on Sabbath.

The purpose of this chapter is to point out that since our attitude toward money and possessions can spell the difference between eternal life and death, then it is certainly appropriate to talk about at least the biblical principles on Sabbath. Number crunching can and should be reserved for another day. But the study of the great principles of Scripture is certainly an ideal Sabbath activity.

To illustrate the significant role money and possessions can play in one's life and the eternal consequences they can have, I want to give you a quick look at several Bible characters who had eternal life in the balance when they made decisions about money. Remember that "these things [situations] occurred as examples, to keep us from setting our hearts on evil things as they did" (1 Corinthians 10:6, NIV).

Individuals in both the Old and New Testaments suffered great harm— even death—as a result of their attitude toward money and possessions. Let's take a look at their stories that Inspiration recorded for us.

Pitching Tents Near Sodom

The events surrounding the destruction of Sodom and Gomorrah tell an amazing account of God's love and justice. The story actually begins in Genesis 12. After Abram and Lot left the city of Ur and followed God's leading toward the Land of Promise, both men became quite wealthy. In those days humanity did not measure wealth by money in the bank or by investments in the stock market, but by flocks of sheep and herds of cattle. Because of their increased need for grazing land, Abram and Lot could no longer live close to each other.

You will remember Abram's offer to Lot. "The whole land is before you. Take your choice. If you go one way, I will go the other." Lot chose the Jordan Valley to the east. After his decision, the Bible records some of the most dreadful words between its covers: "Lot . . . pitched his tents near Sodom" (Genesis 13:12, NIV).

In the next chapter the Bible records that Lot was living in Sodom. Foreign raiding parties attacked and pillaged the cities of Sodom and Gomorrah, taking Lot and his family among their captives. When a messenger brought news of the disaster to Abram, the patriarch could have said, "He made his bed; let him sleep in it." But he didn't. Gathering his 318 trained servants, and through good strategy and the blessing of God, he routed the invaders and rescued the hostages.

Unfortunately, the people from Sodom went right back to the cities, rebuilt them, and began their riotous living habits again. Finally God Himself came down with two angels to see whether or not the reports of the wickedness of Sodom was as bad as He had been told (see Genesis 18:20, 21).

In the days of Abraham it was the practice to leave a gap of several inches between the tent material and the ground. The tent could then shelter its inhabitants from the hot sun yet still allow fresh air to circulate through it by escaping as a breeze through the door. So when God and the angels stopped by Abraham's place on their way to Sodom they found him sitting at the door of his tent "in the air-conditioning" during the heat of the day.

The patriarch invited them in so he could wash their feet and provide them a meal. Hospitality was the fundamental rule of survival in the desert. A person offered food, water, and shelter to others with the understanding that they would provide it to him in turn as he needed it. Following the meal, God announced to Abraham that he and Sarah would be having a son. Then as the visitors prepared to leave, God told the angels to go on to Sodom while He warned Abraham about the city's impending destruction. Of course, Abraham's first thoughts were for the safety of Lot and his family, and so he began bargaining with God to save the righteous in Sodom. Abraham pleaded with God to reduce the number of righteous it would take to spare the city from 50 down to 10. (And Abraham stopped asking before God stopped granting!)

Meanwhile, in the twilight of Sodom's last night, the two angels approached the city. The last evening did not appear any different than the others that had come and gone. Evening fell on a scene of security and prosperity. In the coolness of dusk the people came out to enjoy their pleasure.

The angels entered the city not as mighty heralds of divine judgment but disguised as traveling men looking for a place to spend the night. Fortunately for Lot, he still possessed the spirit of hospitality that he had learned from Abraham. He invited the strangers to his home, and while he was attempting to provide for their needs, the men of Sodom made their lustful demands. Then the angels told Lot and his family who they were and why they had come. They explained that they would save him and all the members of his family who would flee with him from the city.

Lot hurried from home to home of his children with the words "Hurry, we must leave immediately; God is planning to destroy this city tonight!" Sadly, his children and their spouses laughed at him. When Lot returned from his futile visits with his children, "his wife refused to depart without them. The thought of leaving those whom he held dearest on earth seemed more than he could bear. *It was hard to forsake his luxurious home and all the wealth acquired by the labors of his whole life, to go forth a destitute wanderer. . . .* But for the angels of God, they would all have perished in the ruin of Sodom. The heavenly messengers took him and his wife and daughters by the hand and led them out of the city" (*Patriarchs and*

Prophets, p. 160; italics supplied).

As the angels left them and returned to the city to accomplish the task of destruction, God Himself, who had stayed behind to inform Abraham of Sodom's destruction, joined the terrified family and commanded them, "Escape for your life! Do not look behind you nor stay anywhere in the plain; Escape to the mountains, lest you be destroyed" (Genesis 19:17). But Lot, even though the God of heaven was standing beside him and had just assisted his escape from certain death, hesitated in his flight to safety and asked the Lord if he couldn't just go to another little city. And while Lot vacillated, his wife looked back toward the burning city and became a pillar of salt.

"While her body was upon the plain, her heart clung to Sodom, and she perished with it. She rebelled against God *because His judgments involved her possessions* and her children in the ruin. Although so greatly favored in being called out from the wicked city, *she felt that she was severely dealt with, because the wealth that it had taken years to accumulate must be left to destruction.* Instead of thankfully accepting deliverance, she presumptuously looked back to desire the life of those who had rejected the divine warning" (*ibid.*, p. 161; italics supplied).

And what was her husband's fate? "Lot had chosen Sodom for its pleasure and profit. Leaving Abraham's altar and its daily sacrifice to the living God, he had permitted his children to mingle with a corrupt and idolatrous people. . . . He was saved at last as 'a brand plucked out of the fire' (Zechariah 3:2), yet stripped of his possessions, bereaved of his wife and children, dwelling in caves, like the wild beasts, covered with infamy in his old age; and he gave to the world, not a race of righteous men, but two idolatrous nations, at enmity with God and warring upon His people, until, their cup of iniquity being full, they were appointed to destruction. How terrible were the results that followed one unwise step!" (*ibid.*, p. 168).

I wish that space would permit some modern applications of the hard lessons that Lot had to learn. At the very least I would encourage you to read Genesis 19 and chapter 14 of *Patriarchs and Prophets*. One short paragraph will have to suffice here.

"Those who secure for their children worldly wealth and honor at the expense of their eternal interests will find in the end that these advantages are a terrible loss. Like Lot, many see their children ruined, and barely save their own souls. Their lifework is lost; their life is a sad failure. Had they exercised true wisdom, their children might have had less of worldly prosperity, *but they would have made sure of a title to the immortal inheritance*" (*ibid.*, p. 169; italics supplied).

Achan

Joshua 7 records the story of Achan. He had been involved in the successful conquest of Jericho. God had told those who participated in the city's capture not to take any booty for themselves. Everything there was to be considered an offering to Him. However, Achan could not resist keeping some of the spoils for his own use—a beautiful Babylonian garment, 200 shekels or bars of silver, and a wedge of gold. He hid the items in the center of his tent, perhaps thinking that no one would ever discover his shameful deed.

Following the miraculous victory at Jericho, Joshua sent men to conquer the small site of Ai. Though the army of God's people expected a speedy victory at Ai, they were instead routed and lost 36 men in the process.

When the leaders discovered that Achan's selfish act had caused their defeat, they summoned him before them. Although he confessed his wrongful deed, he had to pay the price. He and his entire family were stoned to death and then burned up, along with all their possessions.

"Of the millions of Israel there was but one man who, in that solemn hour of triumph and of judgment, had dared to transgress the command of God. Achan's covetousness was excited by the sight of that costly robe of Shinar; even when it had brought him face to face with death he called it 'a *goodly* Babylonish garment.' One sin had led to another, and he appropriated the gold and silver devoted to the treasury of the Lord—he robbed God of the first fruits of the land of Canaan.

"The deadly sin that led to Achan's ruin had its root in covetousness, of all sins one of the most common and the most lightly regarded. While other offenses meet with detection and punishment, how rarely does the violation of the tenth commandment so much as call forth censure. The enormity of this sin, and its terrible results, are the lessons of Achan's history. . . .

"We have before us the fearful doom of Achan, of Judas, of Ananias and Sapphira. Back of all these we have that of Lucifer, the 'son of the morning,' who, coveting a higher state, forfeited forever the brightness and bliss of heaven. And yet, notwithstanding all these warnings, covetousness abounds.

"Everywhere its slimy track is seen. It creates discontent and dissension in families; it excites envy and hatred in the poor against the rich; it prompts the grinding oppression of the rich toward the poor. And this evil exists not in the world alone, but in the church. How common even here to find selfishness, avarice, overreaching, neglect of charities, and robbery of God 'in tithes and offerings.' Among church members 'in good and regular standing' there are, alas! many Achans. Many a man comes stately to church, and sits at the table of the Lord, while among his possessions are hidden unlawful gains, the things that God has cursed. For a goodly Babylonish garment, multitudes sacrifice the approval of conscience and their hope of heaven. . . .

"Achan's sin brought disaster upon the whole nation. For one man's sin the displeasure of God will rest upon His church till the transgression is searched out and put away. The influence most to be feared by the church is not that of open opposers, infidels, and blasphemers, but on inconsistent professors of Christ. These are the ones who keep back the blessing of the God of Israel and bring weakness upon His people" (*ibid.*, pp. 496, 497).

"If the presence of one Achan was sufficient to weaken the whole camp of Israel, can we be surprised at the little success which attends our efforts when every church and almost every family has its Achan?" (*Testimonies,* vol. 5, p. 157).

You will remember that Achan finally confessed his sin, but unfortunately when it was too late. If we wait until the judgment to acknowledge our overreaching, neglect of charity, and robbery of God in tithes and offerings, our confessions will show only that our punishment is just. I appeal to every reader to ask God's forgiveness for any sins of covetousness that you may have committed in the past, and to ask for His power to overcome such temptations and problems in the future. You need the blessing of God, and so does His church.

Gehazi's Gift for Himself

The miracle of the healing of Naaman in 2 Kings 5 is the setting for the final Old Testament experience. This time it involved a faithful servant of the prophet of God.

After the Lord healed Naaman of his leprosy, he and all his traveling companions returned to Elisha and offered him silver and gold and clothing. (Clothing was expensive and valuable. Most people had only one or two sets of garments at a time.) Elisha refused the gifts in a way that let the Syrian know that it was not any person who had healed him, but the God of Israel. It must have been difficult for Gehazi to see the gifts turned down. Perhaps he thought, *This man wants to make a thank offering of nearly $4 million to the cause of God, which really needs the money, and Elisha is refusing.* After Naaman started back to Syria, Gehazi kept thinking about the sight of all that precious metal and clothing. Remembering his plight as an intern with only one suit and unpaid student loans, he finally determined that he would ask Naaman for a gift for himself.

Gehazi ran to catch up with Naaman, who asked him, "Is everything all right?" The servant then told a lie because of his now-indulged covetousness. Stating that two young men from the school of the prophets were in need, he asked Naaman for a relatively small amount of the wealth the man was carrying back to Syria. Naaman promptly gave him twice as much as he asked for. Hiding the bars of silver, Gehazi planned to use them for himself in the future, but when Elisha confronted him about them, he lied again. Then the prophet revealed to him the details of what his servant had done and stated, "The leprosy of Naaman shall cling to you and your descendants forever" (2 Kings 5:27). To the day of his death he remained a leper, cursed of God and shunned by humanity.

Now, let's look quickly at three similar experiences in the New Testament. The first story about an unnamed man appears in all three Synoptic Gospels. We know him only as the rich young ruler. The Jewish leader had a formidable list of recommendations. He loved Jesus, and Jesus loved him. The young man possessed the qualifications to be a divine force for good. Christ wanted him to be a disciple and offered him a call. In turn he wanted to follow Christ. The rich young ruler was a commandment keeper, he had financial resources, and the public respected him.

But there was one thing wrong. He loved his money more than he loved Jesus. When Christ asked him to use his resources to help others, the Bible says, "He went away sorrowful, for he had great possessions" (Matthew 19:22). All three Synoptic Gospel writers mention that Jesus took this occasion to explain to the disciples that it is not easy for a rich man to enter heaven because those with money always find themselves tempted to trust in it instead of Jesus.

After the young man left, Peter asked Jesus a question that puts things into focus for us. I do not believe that he did it from a selfish motive, because the disciples had already made their commitment to follow Christ without knowing the answer to the question. It was really both a question and a statement: "We have left all and followed You. Therefore what shall we have?" (verse 27). In other words: "What did this man give up by walking away from Your offer?" Jesus answered, "Whoever is willing to leave possessions [houses and lands] or family [parents, siblings, children, spouse] if necessary to follow me, that person will have a hundredfold return in this life and in the end everlasting life" (see verse 29).

"Christ's dealing with the young man is presented as an object lesson. God has given us the rule of conduct which every one of His servants must follow. It is obedience to His law, not merely a legal obedience, but an obedience which enters into the life, and is exemplified in the character. God has set His own standard of character for all who would become subjects of His kingdom. Only those who will become coworkers with Christ, only those who will say, Lord, all I have and all I am is Thine, will be acknowledged as sons and daughters of God. All should consider what it means to desire heaven, and yet to turn away because of the conditions laid down" (*The Desire of Ages*, p. 523).

Just think about what it means to tell Jesus no. That New Testament yuppie said, "No, I can't give You all." What are our lives telling Jesus today?

Following the ascension of Jesus and the outpouring of the Holy Spirit at Pentecost, the disciples of Jesus were filled with zeal and worked intensely to fulfill the gospel commission. In response multitudes believed. Many of the early believers immediately found themselves cut off from their family and friends, and it was necessary for the church to provide them with food and shelter.

"Now the multitude of those who believed were of one heart and one soul; neither did anyone say that any of the things he possessed was his own, but they had all things in common. And with great power the apostles gave witness to the resurrection of the Lord Jesus. And great grace was upon them all. Nor was there anyone among them who lacked; for all who were possessors of lands or houses sold them, and brought the proceeds of the things that were sold, and laid them at the apostles' feet; and they distributed to each as anyone had need" (Acts 4:32-35).

Ananias and Sapphira

The experience of Ananias and Sapphira has left a dark stain upon the history of the early church, however. Along with many others, they felt themselves deeply moved as the apostles preached under the Holy Spirit's power. As a result of the Spirit's influence, they pledged to the Lord's cause the proceeds from the sale of a piece of land.

After the "high" of the meeting they soon gave in to covetousness. They began to regret their promise and even thought that perhaps they had been too hasty and should reconsider their commitment. Talking the matter over, they decided on a new plan. While they would go ahead and sell the land, they would also keep part of the money back for themselves.

If it had been today, the events could have played out like this. On the date of the closing of the sale they deposited the check into their account and had a cashier's check made to the church for part of the money while leaving the remainder in their account. Perhaps one suggested that they celebrate their windfall by going out to the Olive Garden restaurant for a meal. Then they decided that Ananias would deliver the money to the apostles while Sapphira stayed home to phone for reservations and to get herself ready for the night out.

When Ananias brought the money to the apostles, Peter asked him why he had lied to the Holy Ghost. He told the man that once he had promised the land to God, neither the land nor its proceeds were his anymore. "You have lied to God, not us," the apostle said. As soon as he heard that, Ananias dropped dead right in church.

Meanwhile, Sapphira had made the reservations and gotten herself ready to go out, but her husband hadn't come home. Perhaps she thought to herself, *I should have gone myself. Whenever he gets around the brethren, he talks and talks.* So finally after three hours of waiting, she decided to check on Ananias for herself.

When she walked into the church, Peter asked her if they had sold the land for a certain amount—no doubt the amount that Ananias had brought in. "Yes, that's what we got for it," she answered. Then Peter asked her why they had agreed together to test the Holy Spirit. "Those who buried your husband are coming in the door, and they will also carry you out." She also dropped dead in church.

Because she was buried by her husband, they will be together on resurrection day. But which one will it be?

"From the stern punishment meted out to those perjurers, God would have us learn also how deep is His hatred and contempt for all hypocrisy and deception. In pretending that they had given all, Ananias and Sapphira lied to the Holy Spirit, and, as a result, they lost this life and the life that is to come" (*The Acts of the Apostles*, pp. 75, 76).

The entire chapter, "A Warning Against Hypocrisy," gives the details of this story and applies it to our day. In addition, an entire chapter in volume 4 of *Testimonies for the Church*, entitled "Sacredness of Vows," uses the experience to point out our obligations to God, many of which people today completely ignore.

"Everyone is to be his own assessor and is left to give as he purposes in his heart. But there are those who are guilty of the same sin as Ananias and Sapphira, thinking that if they withhold a portion of what God claims in the tithing system the brethren will never know it. Thus thought the guilty couple whose example is given us as a warning. God in this case proves that He searches the heart. The motives and purposes of man cannot be hidden from Him. He has left a perpetual warning to Christians of all ages to beware of the sin to which the hearts of man are continually inclined.

"Although no visible marks of God's displeasure follow the repetition of the sin of Ananias and Sapphira now, yet the sin is just as heinous in the sight of God and will as surely be visited upon the transgressor in the day of judgment, and many will feel the curse of God even in this life" (pp. 469, 470).

I often wonder how the church will ever finish its mission with such great needs and opportunities at a time of worldwide recession and hard times. But Ellen White writes, "If all the tithes of our people flowed into the treasury of the Lord as they should, such blessings would be received that gifts and offerings for sacred purposes would be multiplied tenfold, and thus the channel between God and man would be kept open. The followers of Christ should not wait for thrilling missionary appeals to arouse them to action. If spiritually awake, they would hear in the income of every week, whether much or little, the voice of God and of conscience with authority demanding the tithes and offerings due the Lord.

"Not only are the gifts and labors of Christ's followers desired, but in one sense they are indispensable. All heaven is interested in the salvation of man and waiting for men to become interested in their own salvation and in that of their fellow men. All things are ready, but the church is apparently upon the enchanted ground. *When they shall arouse and lay their prayers, their wealth, and all their energies and resources at the feet of Jesus, the cause of truth will triumph*" (*ibid.*, pp. 474, 475; italics supplied).

The Bible reveals over and over how many have traded eternal life for a pittance of money or possessions. We could mention many more, such as Judas, the rich fool, and Demas. But I want to close this chapter on a much happier note. Many others have made the right decision and set positive examples for us.

Father of the Faithful

I think of Abraham, now known as the father of the faithful, who took the other fork in the road when Lot chose the Jordan Valley. God blessed him and was his protector and provider. He could have built Sarah a mansion to live in, but instead he chose to dwell in a tent to show his family and those about him that this world was not his home.

The Scriptures declare, "By faith he [Abraham] sojourned in the land of promise as in a foreign country, dwelling in tents with Isaac and Jacob, the heirs with him of the same promise; for he waited for the city which has foundations, whose builder and maker is God" (Hebrews 11:9, 10).

"The heritage that God has promised to His people is not in this world. Abraham had no possession in the earth; 'no, not so much as to set his foot on.' Acts 7:5. He possessed great substance, and he used it to the glory of God and the good of his fellow men; but he did not look upon this world as his home. The Lord had called him to leave his idolatrous countrymen, with the promise of the land of Canaan as an everlasting possession; yet neither he nor his son's son received it. When Abraham desired a burial place for his dead, he had to buy it of the Canaanites. His sole possession in the Land of Promise was that rock-hewn tomb in the cave of Machpelah" (*Patriarchs and Prophets*, p. 169).

God's promise to Abraham was not merely the land of Canaan or even our old wicked, polluted planet, but the new earth (see Romans 4:13). God showed him a view of the immortal world, and with this hope he was content. And so we find him in the Bible's hall of faith.

Perhaps no follower of God had a greater temptation to choose worldly wealth and fame than did Moses. He could have been Pharaoh of Egypt with its wealth and luxury, yet he decided to give his all to Jesus.

"By faith Moses, when he became of age, refused to be called the son of Pharaoh's daughter, choosing rather to suffer affliction with the people of God than to enjoy the passing pleasures of sin, esteeming the reproach of Christ greater riches than the treasures in Egypt; for he looked to the reward" (Hebrews 11:24-26).

If you have had the opportunity, as I have, to view the treasures of King Tut's tomb, you know that Moses was not just trading a grass hut and some clay marbles to be with God's people. His decision involved genuine worldly wealth. Instead he chose to be numbered with God's faithful, and now enjoys the company of angels and the heavenly Trinity.

Zacchaeus

Finally a look at one of the most interesting and well-known Bible characters of all will give us courage to make a full surrender to God. Only Luke records the story of Zacchaeus, but everyone who has attended Sabbath school knows the story. Zacchaeus was a Roman tax collector and rich. The Romans had people bid on their tax collecting positions, and the persons who vowed to collect the highest amount of taxes won them. Since the positions paid no salary, the only way to earn a living was to collect even more taxes. It may have been impossible to be an honest tax collector. Such a position was tantamount to extortion. Also Jewish people hated tax collectors because they were fellow countrymen collaborating with the hated occupation power.

But beneath the appearance of worldliness and pride Zacchaeus had a heart susceptible to divine influences. He had heard of Jesus and His love and forgiveness. There awakened in him a longing for a better life. Zacchaeus began to follow the conviction that had taken hold upon him, and to make restitution to those whom he had wronged.

When Zacchaeus got word that Jesus was entering his hometown of Jericho, the little tax collector determined that he must see Him. He ran to the main street where Jesus would pass, only to encounter a large crowd gathered along the road. It was like the Tournament of Roses Parade, only on a smaller scale. Since he was a short man even in his day, he decided to climb a tree—the chief IRS man climbed a tree!

Then several miracles happened in quick succession. First, Jesus stopped right under the tree where Zacchaeus was sitting. Then He looked up in the branches, and even though they had never met before, He called Zacchaeus by name. And though you or I would never think of doing so, Jesus invited Himself home for dinner. Zacchaeus was thrilled. He surrendered his heart to Jesus, and as a result of that visit he volunteered to make fourfold restitution to those he had wronged and to give half of his goods to the poor. And Jesus said, "Today salvation has come to this house" (Luke 19:9).

So there we have it—examples of real people. Some lost their way and some made good decisions. In which group will we be found? It seems to go without saying that if one can lose eternal life over money and possessions, then he or she should study the subject carefully and choose the road taken by those who have set their affections on things above.

APPLICATION
Chapter 2

1. Can you name other biblical characters that made serious decisions about money and possessions?

2. Ellen White calls the experience of Achan "one in a million." What do you think the ratio of Achans to faithful people is today?

3. Can we expect God's blessing and the outpouring of His Holy Spirit in latter-rain power while we are serving the world?

4. The story of salvation history is only partially recorded in the Scriptures. It is still being written in heaven. What will it say about you?

—————◆—————

CHAPTER THREE

"Trust in the Lord with all your heart, and lean not on your own understanding;

"In all your ways acknowledge Him, and He shall direct your paths.

"Do not be wise in your own eyes; fear the Lord and depart from evil.

"It will be health to your flesh, and strength to your bones.

"Honor the Lord with your possessions, and with the firstfruits of all your increase;

"So your barns will be filled with plenty, and your vats will overflow with new wine" (Proverbs 3:5-10).

Putting God First

The passage quoted above indicates that if I will trust God with all my heart and put Him first in my finances, then He will direct me (give me wisdom) and bless my efforts (provide for my needs). What person or family could afford to be without God's wisdom and blessing?

Why should God be first? Is it just because He has the authority to demand it? One thing for sure is that He doesn't need the money. I believe that there are a number of important reasons we could list that it is for our best good to put God ahead of everything else.

Putting God first helps us to place life in proper perspective. It enables us to recognize that we look to God for our security and not to our talents or possessions. Furthermore, it allows God's blessing to extend our service.

Basic Principles

Five basic principles help us to understand the biblical perspective of personal money management. I will share them with you in this chapter, enlarging on several of them briefly here and then addressing the others in chapters of their own. The principles are:

1. God is the owner of everything.

2. Our purpose in life is to glorify God.

3. The tithe is the minimum testimony of our Christian commitment.

4. Debt is bad.

5. Prosperity is having what you need when you need it.

God's ownership is a concept that everyone gives lip service to, but few really understand and even fewer practice it. Before I had studied the subject in some detail I was willing to give God ownership of the national parks, the oceans from the territorial boundaries on out, and perhaps even the grassy strip in the middle of the interstate highways. But to recognize God as the owner of all I possess and to feel that I owed Him some accountability beyond the tithe had never dawned on me. I have been rather proud of the fact that I worked my own way through academy (milking cows from 3:00 a.m. to 7:00 a.m., going to school all day, and then milking the same cows from 3:00 to 7:00 in the evening), college, and graduate school. Nobody ever gave me anything. I got what I have by working for it. So how could God say that He is the owner of everything?

"Some think that only a portion of their means is the Lord's. When they have set apart a portion for religious and charitable purposes, they regard the remainder as their own, to be used as they see fit. But in this they mistake. All we possess is the Lord's, and we are accountable to Him for the use we make of it" (*Christ's Object Lessons*, p. 351).

In addition, the Bible contains numerous references to God's ownership based both on creation and redemption. For example:

"The earth is the Lord's, and all its fullness, the world and those who dwell therein" (Psalm 24:1).

"If I were hungry, I would not tell you; for the world is Mine, and all its fullness" (Psalm 50:12).

David and the Temple

We see this principle illustrated in the experience of David and the building of the sanctuary later known as Solomon's Temple. David was sitting in the palace Scripture calls his house of cedar, perhaps in his library contemplating the blessings of God. He thought to himself, *I live in this beautiful house while God is still dwelling in the tent church that we carried through the wilderness.* So he said to himself, *I will build a representative place for the God of heaven to dwell among us.*

The next time David saw the prophet Nathan, he told him of his plan, and Nathan said that "it sounds like a good idea to me." Later when the prophet talked with God, the Lord told him that David should not build the Temple because he was a man of war and had blood on his hands. When Nathan relayed the message to the king, David was disappointed but decided to ask God if he could just draw the plans and get the material together. The Lord accepted his request, and David began work. He drew the plans, prepared a materials list, and did the cost estimate. It was all more elaborate than anything that anyone had ever built for God before.

The people responded to David's leadership, and soon the funds were raised, the craftsmen hired, and the material for the Temple brought from far and near to Jerusalem. Although people call it Solomon's Temple, it was actually his father David who conceived the idea, drew the plans, raised the money, bought the materials, hired the craftsmen, and prepared the site. When Solomon began his work, the building was just like a log home kit— all precut and numbered, ready to be assembled.

When David had completed his work of preparation, he called the people of Israel together for a celebration. He held a service of praise to God and during it he offered a prayer of thanksgiving to God recorded in 1 Chronicles 29. I will quote just a portion of it here to show you David's understanding of God's ownership. "Now therefore, our God, we thank You and praise Your glorious name. But who am I, and who are my people, that we should be able to offer so willingly as this? For all things come from You, and of our own we have given You. For we are aliens and pilgrims before You, as were all our fathers; our days on earth are as a shadow, and without hope. O Lord our God, all this abundance that we have prepared to build You a house for Your holy name is from Your hand, and is all Your own" (verses 13-16).

David was saying in effect, "We really can't take any credit for this accomplishment because we are really just giving You back Your own stuff." The whole thing reminds me of how on several occasions when our daughter Melissa was younger she came to me and said she needed money. When I asked her what she planned to do with the money, she would say, "I would like to buy you and Mom a gift." It's the idea that counts.

God's Ownership

This principle of understanding God's ownership applies to business management as well.

"Even in this age of passion for money getting, when competition is so sharp and methods are so unscrupulous, it is still widely acknowledged that, for a young man starting in life, integrity, diligence, temperance, purity, and thrift constitute a better capital than any amount of mere money.

"Yet even of those who appreciate the value of these qualities and acknowledge the Bible as their source, there are but few who recognize the principle upon which they depend.

"That which lies at the foundation of business integrity and of true success is the recognition of God's ownership. The Creator of all things, He is the original proprietor. We are His stewards. All that we have is a trust from Him, to be used according to His direction" (*Education*, p. 137).

"Money is not ours; houses and grounds, pictures and furniture, garments and luxuries, do not belong to us. We are pilgrims, we are strangers. We have only a grant of those things that are necessary for health and life. . . . Our temporal blessings are given us in trust, to prove whether we can be entrusted with eternal riches. If we endure the proving of God, then we shall receive that purchased possession which is to be our own—

glory, honor, and immortality" (*The Adventist Home*, p. 367).

To be successful as a Christian money manager we must understand the principle of God's ownership. Perhaps an illustration from the law will assist in making the point. In real property law—real estate—we encounter the concept of adverse possession, in which over a period of years (20 in most jurisdictions) ownership passes from one party to another without the need or use of a written document. No deed passes between the parties. Very simply, adverse possession can take place when a party, not the true owner, begins to act like the owner of a certain piece of land. This individual tells people he or she owns the land in question, and may build a fence around it. Perhaps this person may keep it up by mowing the fields, and even pay the taxes on it. During this time, if the true owner does nothing to refute such owner-like actions of the other party, then title to the land can pass to the other party by adverse possession. We get this idea from English common law.

But God's law or economy does not know any such thing as adverse possession. We can behave like owners for 20 years or all our lives, but God still remains the owner. At our death we must lay it all down and then give an account to Him of how we used it.

During Old Testament times you could buy land but you could not keep it. Every 49 years on the year of jubilee all property went back to the original owners or families.

Our Relationship to God

It is interesting to note people's relationship to God in Scripture.

God is the Shepherd—we are the sheep.

God is our Father—we are His children.

God is eternal—we are like vapor.

God is the Creator—we are creatures.

God is the Vine—we are the branches.

God is the Head—we are the body.

And in financial matters:

God is the Master—we are His stewards.

Scripture depicts the position of a steward as one of great responsibility. A steward is the supreme authority for all under the master and has full responsibility for all the master's possessions, household affairs, and even raising the children. Remember Abraham told his steward Eliezer, "Go, find a wife for my son."

Once we understand this first principle—God's ownership—then we can make the other business or financial decisions of our lives with spiritual maturity and confidence. For example, when we recognize that God is really the true owner of all we possess, at our death what should we do with what we did not use? The answer is simple. Give it back to Him! We will discuss this in more detail in chapter 10.

The second principle is a simple one that Scripture repeats again and again. It is that our purpose in life is to glorify God, not to accumulate possessions. Not to be famous. Just simply to glorify God.

"Therefore, whether you eat or drink, or whatever you do, do all to the glory of God" (1 Corinthians 10:31).

"Let your light so shine before men, that they may see your good works and glorify your Father in heaven" (Matthew 5:16).

I believe that the "good works" and "whatever you do" spoken of in the verses quoted above also include the management of our money. As we all know, our checkbook records have a lot to say about the nature of our lives.

The third principle involves the tithe. Tithe is the minimum testimony of our Christian commitment. It is not an offering, but a vow we make to God at our conversion and baptism as we enter into covenant relationship with Him. The next chapter will deal with the tithe principle in more detail.

The fourth principle tells us that debt is bad. I realize that sounds like an extremely simplistic statement, but I will repeat it—debt is bad. Chapter 5 discusses this topic in a way that will greatly assist many families seeking relief from debt. I believe this chapter is one of the most valuable in the book.

Finally, the fifth principle lets us know what God means when He says, "Beloved, I pray that you may prosper in all things and be in health, just as your soul prospers" (3 John 2).

From the biblical perspective, prosperity is having what you need when you need it. It is not the accumulation of possessions. Prosperity is claiming the promise of God in Philippians 4:19: "And my God shall supply all your need according to His riches in glory by Christ Jesus."

True Bible religion is not a "name it and claim it" relationship with God. He does not promise His followers that they will all be rich. In fact, He says that all who live godly lives shall suffer persecution. What He does offer is better than any worldly wealth. He says, "I will supply your needs, and wherever you go I will be with you." Then in the end He will give His faithful ones true wealth and responsibility and eternal life. I want to claim these promises and thank Him for them. How about you?

APPLICATION
Chapter 3

1. How can we really put God first in our lives and demonstrate in a practical way that He is the owner of everything?

2. Has God ever failed to supply your need? If so, explain the circumstances.

3. Explain why just living from paycheck to paycheck is not an appropriate lifestyle and financial management system for a Christian.

4. The five basic principles given in this chapter are valuable only as we apply them to our lives. Take a few minutes and review the principles, and then see how they compare to your present situation.

———◆———

CHAPTER FOUR

"The love of money, the desire for wealth, is the golden chain that binds [people] to Satan" (Steps to Christ, *p. 44*).

Satan's Plan for Your Money

Few realize that selfishness—materialism—lies at the very heart of the conflict between good and evil. A number of years ago God gave Ellen White a vision of one of Satan's counsel meetings. Outlining his strategy for the last days, he counseled his angels as to the most successful plan for overcoming the faith of God's people. Among other things he said, "Go, make the possessors of lands and money drunk with the cares of this life. Present the world before them in its most attractive light, that they may lay up their treasure here and fix their affections upon earthly things. We must do our utmost to prevent those who labor in God's cause from obtaining means to use against us. . . . Make them care more for money than for the upbuilding of Christ's kingdom and the spread of the truths we hate, and we need not fear their influence; for we know that every selfish, covetous person will fall under our power, and will finally be separated from God's people" (*Testimonies to Ministers,* p. 474).

Many assume that they can trust God for their eternal life but that they are on their own when it comes to the present life and its needs. Accordingly, our natural tendency is to hoard money and to always want more.

The Tithing System

To help individuals to overcome selfishness and materialism, God instituted the tithing system. Of course, with the statement we quoted from *Testimonies to Ministers* fresh in our minds, it is easy to see that Satan would not like this plan of systematic support for God's church. Believe it or not, a committee at the General Conference did not develop the tithing system whereby one returns a tenth of his or her increase right off the top to God. In addition, God doesn't need the money for as Psalm 50:12 tells us: "If I were hungry, I would not tell you, For the world is Mine, and all its fullness." The real purpose of the tithing system as Moses noted when he reviewed God's laws with Israel was "that you may learn to fear the Lord your God always" (Deuteronomy 14:23).

With all the discussion regarding tithe today, one could write an entire book on the subject. And no book on Christian money management would be complete without at least a chapter on the principle of tithing. In my judgment it is the very foundation of Christian commitment and therefore the point at which I begin all my Christian financial counseling. Really, the tithe is the minimum testimony of our Christian commitment. Nowhere in the Bible do we find any indication that God's portion is less than a tenth.

Do you tithe? If you do, why? How much are you to tithe? Do you like to tithe? Are there any benefits to tithing?

I find that a vast majority of Christians today know little about the tithe or its purpose. Some mistakenly feel that since tithing is not a test of membership, it is optional or only for those who can afford it. Is tithing really just a matter of conscience? Yes, conscience does play a role in tithing. Its part concerns not whether or not one should tithe, but how much the honest tithe is. "Of the means which is entrusted to man, God claims a certain portion—a tithe; but He leaves all free to say how much the tithe is, and whether or not they will give more than this" (*Testimonies*, vol. 5, p. 149). Unfortunately, even many churches view tithing as simply a funding scheme to help the church meet its budget. Pastors seldom teach its biblical purpose. Many regard getting people to tithe as a rarely won uphill battle.

Yet I have found that those individuals who do understand the concept of tithing are excited about returning it to God. They do not—as others often do—give grudgingly, out of a sense of obligation and pressure.

The word "tithe" means one tenth. Tithing is simply giving 10 percent of your income to God. All we have belongs to Him in the first place. His request is that we give only 10 percent back to Him, and then we manage and distribute the other 90 percent.

Actually it is a tremendous privilege and honor! God trusts you so much that He allows you the responsibility and privilege of managing 90 percent and returning only 10 percent to Him through His church. You are, of course, free to give much more, but that is all your covenant or contract with God calls for. I'll discuss more about the contract later in this chapter.

Tithing in the Bible

To have a better understanding of the tithe, let's take a quick look at its history from God's Word.

The first tithe recorded in Scripture was given more than 4,000 years ago—more than 400 years before God gave the law to Moses. Abraham had returned from a successful hostage rescue mission to save his nephew Lot, his family, and the other people captured from Sodom. The king of

Sodom was so grateful for the rescue that he offered Abram (his name hadn't been changed yet) "the goods"—all the spoils of the war. Abram responded that he had lifted his hand to the Lord—made a covenant with God (see Genesis 14:22)—that he would take nothing from anyone. Then he did two notable things. First he tithed of all the spoil to Melchizedek, the priest of the most high God, and then he gave all the remainder back to the people of Sodom—thereby storing it up in heaven, as we will learn in chapter 10.

Even though Abram was living in a tent, he stated that he had no use for the money. He simply tithed it and handed back the rest to the people who needed it more than he did.

Abram gave Melchizedek a tenth of all he had won in the battle that day. Out of gratitude to God, he offered it freely and willingly. Melchizedek never requested it. Abram simply offered it. As I see it, Abram really gave God—by way of Melchizedek—his part of the covenant bargain as an expression of his gratitude for His divine leadership in the battle.

Immediately after this experience the Lord came to Abram in a vision and said, "Do not be afraid, Abram. I am your shield, your exceedingly great reward" (Genesis 15:1). In effect the Lord was telling Abram that He, God, would be his protector and provider—and He was.

The next example we have of tithing occurs in Genesis 28. Jacob had to flee his home because he had tricked Esau out of his birthright. Resting one night during his journey, he dreamed of a staircase that reached from earth to heaven. Angels of God went up and down the staircase.

In the dream, God appeared to Jacob and promised him the land he was sleeping upon, many thousands of descendants, and protection wherever he went. When he awoke the next morning, Jacob built an altar on the spot. "Then Jacob made a vow, saying, 'If God will be with me, and keep me in this way that I am going, and give me bread to eat and clothing to put on, so that I come back to my father's house in peace, then the Lord shall be my God. And this stone which I have set as a pillar shall be God's house, and of all that You give me I will surely give a tenth to You' " (Genesis 28:20-22).

Here again, Jacob took the initiative to commit 10 percent of his income to God. The Lord did not demand it of him. Instead, the patriarch willingly offered it, choosing to put God first in his life and demonstrating his commitment with his tithe.

Years later when God presented His law to His people in written form, He included the provision of tithing. By now God's promise to Jacob in Genesis 28 had become reality.

At the time of the Exodus, God again declared the law of the tithe and the law of the central storehouse in Deuteronomy 12 and 14. "But when you cross over the Jordan and dwell in the land which the Lord your God is giving you to inherit, and He gives you rest from all your enemies round about, so that you dwell in safety, then there will be a place where the Lord your God chooses to make His name abide. There you shall bring all that I command you: your burnt offerings, your sacrifices, your tithes, the heave offerings of your hand, and all your choice offerings which you vow to the Lord. . . . Take heed to yourself that you do not offer your burnt offerings in every place that you see; but in the place which the Lord chooses, in one of your tribes, there you shall offer your burnt offerings, and there you shall do all that I command you" (Deuteronomy 12:10-14).

"And all the tithe of the land, whether of the seed of the land or of the fruit of the tree, is the Lord's. It is holy to the Lord" (Leviticus 27:30).

"You shall truly tithe all the increase of your grain that the field produces year by year. And you shall eat before the Lord your God, in the place where He chooses to make His name abide, the tithe of your grain and your new wine and your oil, of the firstlings of your herds and your flocks, that you may learn to fear the Lord your God always" (Deuteronomy 14:22, 23).

We all recognize that when Israel obeyed God, He blessed them, and when they disobeyed, they inherited curses. Obedience brought prosperity. They were the head and not the tail, lending to others but not borrowing themselves. On the other hand, when they disobeyed God's commands, they became the tail and not the head and ended up in debt, having to borrow from other nations (see Deuteronomy 28).

Finally Israel got further and further from God. Many were not bringing their full tithe to the Temple storehouse. Some no longer tithed at all. This was the setting for the third chapter of Malachi—and also parallel testimony for our day, because the chapter has as its context preparation for the coming of the Lord.

Over and over we are told to "study the third chapter of Malachi." Let's take a look at the pertinent part of it now.

"'For I am the Lord, I do not change; therefore you are not consumed, O sons of Jacob. Yet from the days of your fathers you have gone away from My ordinances and have not kept them. Return to Me, and I will return to you,' says the Lord of hosts. 'But you said, "In what way shall we return?" Will a man rob God? Yet you have robbed Me! But you say, "In what way have we robbed You?" In tithes and offerings. You are cursed with a curse, for you have robbed Me, even this whole nation. Bring all the tithes into the storehouse, that there may be food in My house, and prove Me now in this,' says the Lord of hosts, 'if I will not open for you the windows of heaven and pour out for you such blessing that there will not be room enough to receive it. And I will rebuke the devourer for your sakes, so that he will not destroy the fruit of your ground, nor shall the vine fail to bear fruit for you in the field,' says the Lord of hosts; 'and all nations will call you blessed, for you will be a delightful land,' says the Lord of hosts" (Malachi 3:6-12).

It seems clear to me that what the Lord states here is that if the people want to take their curses and make them into blessings, then they will have to uphold the law of the central storehouse of Deuteronomy 12 and bring all their tithe to God's house.

Simply stated, an honest tithe is the whole tithe to the right place. Years ago when my family moved to the South I first encountered the expression "y'all" that people use interchangeably with the plural of "you." As one reads Malachi 3:10 in the King James Version, one could believe that the author was from the South when he said, "Bring ye all the tithes into the storehouse." A more proper translation would be "Bring all the tithe into the storehouse" or "Bring the whole tithe into the storehouse."

This, then, is the history and law of the tithe. "The New Testament does not reenact the law of the tithe, as it does not that of the Sabbath; for the validity of both is assumed, and their deep spiritual import explained. . . . While we as a people are seeking faithfully to give God the time which He has reserved as His own, shall we not also render to Him that portion of our means which He claims?" (*Counsels on Stewardship*, p. 66).

Tithing is very important to God, as Scripture states in so many places. As I close this chapter, let me share with you just a few of the reasons that led me to conclude that the tithe is foundational to religious experience.

The May 14 and July 9, 1992, *Adventist Review*s noted the great news of recent baptisms in the formerly closed country of Albania. "By the end of the three-week meetings [in Tirana, Albania] 32 people were baptized, including Meropi Gjika, . . . who had waited 51 years for the opportunity.

"Gjika embraced the gospel truth as a result of the preaching of Albanian-born Daniel Lewis, an Adventist missionary sent by the church from Boston, Massachusetts in 1930. She joined a company of 12 initial converts but could not be baptized then. Though she has lived through decades of adversity and persecution, her faith has survived." And her stewardship commitment remained undaunted. "Although she had received a pension of only $4 per month for the past 20 years, she had saved her tithes all those years."

Why did she save her tithe all these years? I mean, really, tithing isn't even a test of faith in the Adventist Church.

According to a study done by Roger Dudley at Andrews University for the NAD Church Ministries Department, 46 to 51 percent of North American Adventists do not tithe. And we aren't being persecuted. What is the real story on tithing? Is tithing optional?

Independent Ministries

You have seen a lot lately in the Adventist press about independent ministries and how some are accepting tithe. The *Adventist Review* and many union papers have contained articles on the subject. Are we just making a mountain out of a molehill? What is the big problem?

Over the past few years I have had the opportunity to study and teach in the area of the biblical principles of personal money management. And now as a result of my work with Adventist-Laymen's Services and Industries (ASI) I have studied even deeper into the tithe issue. Obviously, I won't have space to share a great deal in this chapter, but I would like to give you just a peek at some interesting things I have discovered.

The reason that tithing is not a test of faith is that God has specified one tenth of the increase. The church leaves the true amount of one's increase to the conscience of the individual. However, God has laid out the tithing plan clearly enough for all who desire to understand (see *Testimonies*, vol. 3, p. 394). In fact, Ellen White tells us that "the new converts should be fully enlightened as to their duty to return to the Lord His own. The command to pay tithe is so plain that there is no semblance of excuse for disregarding it" (*Counsels on Stewardship*, p. 105).

In addition, she states on the same page, in the context of teaching about the duty to tithe, "God would be better pleased to have six thoroughly converted to the truth than to have sixty make a profession and yet not be truly converted."

Importance of Tithing

Probably the strongest language Ellen White used in regard to teaching tithing appears in the following quotation: "If they [pastors] fail to set before the church the importance of returning to God His own, if they do not see to it that the officers under them are faithful, and that the tithe is brought in, they are in peril. . . . They should be relieved of their responsibility" (*ibid.*, p. 106). And even stronger: " 'Unfaithful servant' is written against their names in the books of heaven" (*Testimonies*, vol. 4, p. 256).

Why so serious? Let me share with you just four reasons. (We could list many more.)

1. The tree of knowledge of good and evil is equivalent to tithing.

From earliest times humanity has been involved with God in a stewardship relationship. While in the Garden of Eden human beings were to have full dominion and could eat of all the trees except one. Of that only

God had said, "Don't eat of it, or you will die" (see Genesis 2:17).

It was a visible, tangible way of demonstrating their allegiance to and dependence upon God. After humanity's fall and expulsion from the Garden, God used tithes and offerings as the visible demonstration of their dependence upon Him.

"The Lord placed our first parents in the Garden of Eden. He surrounded them with everything that could minister to their happiness, and He bade them acknowledge Him as the possessor of all things. In the garden He caused to grow every tree that was pleasant to the eye or good for food; but among them He made one reserve. Of all else, Adam and Eve might freely eat; but of this one tree God said, 'Thou shalt not eat of it.' Here was the test of their gratitude and loyalty to God.

"So the Lord has imparted to us heaven's richest treasure in giving us Jesus. With Him He has given us all things richly to enjoy. The productions of the earth, the bountiful harvests, the treasures of gold and silver, are His gifts. Houses and lands, food and clothing, He has placed in the possession of men. He asks us to acknowledge Him as the Giver of all things; and for this reason He says, Of all your possessions I reserve a tenth for Myself, besides gifts and offerings, which are to be brought into My storehouse. This is the provision God has made for carrying forward the work of the gospel" (*Counsels on Stewardship*, p. 65; see also *Seventh-day Adventists Believe . . .* , p. 271).

Did you know that just as the devil appeared to Eve in the tree to deceive her in regard to God's authority and her dependence upon Him, He will also work hard in the last days "to deceive, if possible, the very elect" in regard to the tithe—man's present test? Ellen White recorded this fact in a letter she wrote to Mr. and Mrs. S. N. Haskell on December 17, 1908 (*Manuscript Releases*, vol. 19, pp. 376, 377). The letter is entitled "The Workings of Satan; Use of Tithe." Note the following two paragraphs:

"The time has come when the tithes and offerings belonging to the Lord are to be used in accomplishing a decided work. They are to be brought into the treasury to be used in an orderly way to sustain the gospel laborers in their work. In Malachi 3:10 we read, 'Bring ye all the tithes into the storehouse, that there may be meat in mine house, and prove me now herewith, saith the Lord of hosts, if I will not open you the windows of heaven, and pour you out a blessing, that there shall not be room enough to receive it.'

"Satan is rallying his forces and seeking to bring in heresies to confuse the minds of those who have not been trained to understand the leadings of the Holy Spirit. *A delusive net is being prepared for them, and those who have been warned again and again, but have not educated themselves to understand the warnings, surely will be taken in Satan's snare*" (italics supplied).

Let me tell you, my friends, the old snake is in the tree again, and this time he is saying, "God really didn't mean that you had to turn all your tithe in through your local church or conference. The church is in a terrible apostasy. Do you think God would want you to support apostasy with your tithe? I don't think so either. Why don't you just send it to where you think it will do the most good?"

Have you heard such snake talk recently? Don't be deceived by it.

"God's reserved resources are to be used in no such haphazard way. The tithe is the Lord's, and those who meddle with it will be punished with the loss of their heavenly treasure unless they repent. Let the work no longer be hedged up because the tithe has been diverted into various channels other than the *one* to which the Lord has said it should go. Provision is to be made for these other lines of work. They are to be sustained, but *not* from the tithe. God has not changed; the tithe is still to be used for the support of the ministry" (*Testimonies*, vol. 9, pp. 249, 250; italics supplied).

By the way, do you know why Eve ate of the tree?

Was she just eating between meals?

"There was nothing poisonous in the fruit itself, and the sin was not merely in yielding to appetite. It was distrust of God's goodness, disbelief of His Word, and rejection of His authority that made our first parents transgressors, and that brought into the world a knowledge of evil" (*Education*, p. 25).

2. Tithing is our part of the covenant relationship with God.

A covenant is an agreement between two or more people. Scripture has much to say about the covenant or agreement between God and man. "He who gave His only-begotten Son to die for you has made a covenant with you. He gives you His blessings, and in return He requires you to bring Him your tithes and offerings" (*Counsels on Stewardship*, p. 75).

This contract is a bilateral one in which both parties make promises. If only God acted and made promises and not humanity, then we would have a unilateral contract. Such a unilateral contract on God's part would mean everyone would be saved. Jesus died for all, but not all will be saved because some decline God's offer of salvation and refuse to live a life in harmony with His revealed will.

As we discussed earlier in this chapter, Abraham was a faithful tither as part of his relationship to God. Jacob also responded to God's promise of protection and blessing by vowing to be faithful in his tithing.

In the most well-known scriptural passage on tithe—Malachi 3:6-12—

God says, in essence, "If you will return to Me and be faithful in your tithes and offerings, I will change the curse that has been on you for robbing Me. I will open for you the windows of heaven and pour you out such a blessing that you will not have room enough to receive it." In addition, He promised protection for crops and a blessing on the land.

Again we see here a bilateral contract: "If you do this, I will do that."

"In the third chapter of Malachi is found the contract God has made with man" (Ellen G. White in *Review and Herald*, Dec. 17, 1901).

As members of God's remnant church we have made a covenant or agreement with God just as did Abraham and Jacob.

Every time I see a baptism I remember my own. My older brother, Ken, and I were baptized together after attending the pastor's Bible class and studying a Voice of Prophecy junior correspondence course. The pastor went over the fundamental Adventist beliefs with us, and then explained that he would examine the baptismal candidates publicly before the congregation. On the Sabbath that I was baptized in that farm pond just north of Fort Bragg, California, the pastor requested that we come forward. He as a typical pastor asked us 13 questions. One of them went something like this: "Do you believe that the Seventh-day Adventist Church is the remnant church of Bible prophecy, and is it your purpose to support it with your tithe and offerings?" When I said yes, I didn't have my fingers crossed behind my back. I meant it then, and I still mean it today. That was part of my baptismal vow. I still want God to know that He can count on me to be faithful in this regard.

How about your baptismal vows today? Are you being faithful to them?

3. Failure to be faithful in tithing is robbery of God (Malachi 3:8, 9).

Have you ever thought this one through? Most of us would never think of stealing from anyone, but would we rob our Creator, God?

I believe that I can best illustrate the seriousness of robbery through a look at modern criminal law. If I were to take something that doesn't belong to me, I would be guilty of one of several different possible crimes.

For sake of illustration, let's say the item I want from you is a new bicycle—an 18-speed mountain bike. If you leave the bike parked in your driveway while you head for town on an errand, and I stop and take it with me, what am I guilty of? Theft. I took the personal property of another with the intent to deprive the rightful owner of it.

Suppose, however, before you leave for town you lock the bike in your house. Then I come along, break into your home, and steal the bike. What crime am I guilty of? Burglary. I broke into and entered the dwelling of another with the purpose of committing a felony therein (stealing your bike).

Now the situation gets more serious and complicated. Imagine that I should see you riding your bike one day, wave you down, then seize it from you without your permission and threaten to harm you if you don't comply. What crime would I be guilty of then? This is robbery. In modern Western criminal law robbery is when the one harmed is present and does not give permission or consent for the item to be taken. It is larceny from the person or presence of another usually by violence or threat, but always without the owner's consent.

Is God present when we take His tithe?

"And there is no creature hidden from His sight, but all things are naked and open to the eyes of Him to whom we must give account" (Hebrews 4:13).

Does God give His permission for us to use His tithe, or does He have plans for it?

"God lays His hand upon all man's possessions, saying: I am the owner of the universe, and these goods are Mine. The tithe you have withheld I reserve for the support of My servants in their work of opening the Scriptures to those who are in the regions of darkness, who do not understand My law. *In using My reserve fund to gratify your own desires you have robbed souls of the light which I made provision for them to receive.* You have had opportunity to show loyalty to Me, but you have not done this. You have robbed Me; you have stolen My reserve fund. 'Ye are cursed with a curse'" (*Testimonies*, vol. 6, p. 387; italics supplied).

Also speaking in the context of the judgment, Ellen White tells us, "Many names are enrolled on the church book that have robbery recorded against them in the Ledger of Heaven. And unless these repent and work for the Master with disinterested benevolence, they will certainly share in the doom of the unfaithful steward" (*Testimonies*, vol. 4, pp. 481, 482).

4. Tithing is an act of worship.

Malachi 3:10 tells us to bring our tithe, not to send it. "Bring all the tithes . . ."—bring the whole tithe. Nor has God asked us to distribute the tithe—only to take it to the storehouse as an act of worship.

The only offering that Jesus ever commended was that from the widow who gave everything she had to a corrupt church. A church that was preparing to kill Him. But she had brought her offering as an act of worship. "Jesus understood her motive. She believed the service of the Temple to be of God's appointment, and she was anxious to do her utmost to sustain it" (*The Desire of Ages*, p. 615).

Commenting on this incident and the sacrifices of the poor in general, Ellen White stated, "Even though the means thus consecrated be misapplied, so that it does not accomplish the object which the donor had in view—the glory of God and the salvation of souls—those who made the sacrifice in sincerity of soul, with an eye single to the glory of God, will not lose their reward" (*Testimonies*, vol. 2, p. 519).

In the context of encouraging public worship, she counseled, "Leave your home cares, and come to find Jesus, and He will be found of you. Come with your offerings as God has blessed you. Show your gratitude to your Creator, the Giver of all your benefits, by a freewill offering. *Let none who are able come empty-handed.* 'Bring ye all the tithes into the storehouse, that there may be meat in mine house, and prove me now herewith, saith the Lord of hosts, if I will not open you the windows of heaven, and pour you out a blessing, that there shall not be room enough to receive it' " (*ibid.,* p. 576).

Now I am beginning to see why Meropi Gjika saved her tithe all those years. And why it was such a happy day for her when she was baptized and officially joined the family of God.

I believe that she had decided not to eat of the forbidden fruit, though no doubt sorely tempted to do so over those many years.

I believe that she cherished her covenant with God.

I believe that she had determined that she would not rob God.

But most of all, I believe that she was echoing the words of the psalmist in Psalm 116:12-14:

"What shall I render to the Lord for all His benefits toward me?

I will take up the cup of salvation, and call upon the name of the Lord,

I will pay my vows to the Lord *now* in the presence of all His people."

So why all the fuss about tithing? Does God need the money? According to Psalm 50, He doesn't. However, the church does, *but not nearly as much as our people need the blessings.*

Tithing is important to me because it is important to God. I want God to know that I trust His goodness, believe His Word, and accept His authority. I want Him to know that He has first place in my life.

How about you?

This chapter completes the spiritual implications section of the book, though it has only laid the foundation of the biblical principles of personal money management. In the next section we will learn how to get out of and stay out of debt. I will give you an example of how a Christian family can set up a budget that will work. We will look at ways to train children that will enable them to avoid the pitfalls that we adults have fallen into. And I will give you many suggestions on how to make the biggest and most expensive purchase of your life—your home.

APPLICATION
Chapter 4

1. What problems develop in my relationship to God if I fail to return an honest tithe?

2. What would happen to God's church if all of His professed followers returned an honest tithe?

3. Can I be the judge and use my own discretion as to where I return my tithe? If you answer yes, what support from Inspiration could you give?

4. Will you join me in renewing your covenant relationship with God by reaffirming your commitment to faithful tithing?

◆

"Train up a child in the way he should go, and when he is old he will not depart from it. "The rich rules over the poor, and the borrower is servant [slave] to the lender" (Proverbs 22:6, 7).

The Tyranny of Debt

Many biblical descriptions of what the world will be like just before Christ returns indicate that people will be what we call materialistic. "But know this, that in the last days perilous times will come: for men will be lovers of themselves [selfish], lovers of money [materialistic], boasters, proud, . . . lovers of pleasure rather than lovers of God" (2 Timothy 3:1-4).

In this materialistic, money-oriented society, men and women place a high priority on possessions, earning power, and lifestyle. Those who cannot afford to live as they would like to will borrow or go into debt to secure those things that they feel they must have. Even the apparently wealthy have heavy debt loads that threaten to swamp them. Donald Trump with his investments in real estate in Atlantic City is leveraged in debt up to the very limits of his ability to pay.

Borrowing on the Future

A person or a family living in debt—on borrowed money—is really living today on funds expected to be earned in the future. If any life changes occur, then serious financial embarrassment can result. Many feel that bankruptcy is their only option at that point. (A little later in this chapter I will discuss bankruptcy from the Christian perspective.)

Let's look at problems that debt can lead to. A husband and wife both working can bring in a relatively large income. Often they will begin purchasing items they believe go with their lifestyle. The problems develop when circumstances change. The wife may get pregnant and for a period of time be unable to work. Or one (or both in a worst-case scenario) may get laid off or have his or her position terminated. In either situation a couple's financial condition deteriorates rapidly. They begin all kinds of desperate measures: bill consolidation loans, with their high interest; borrowing from relatives; second mortgages; etc. A family now faces great stress, and not infrequently this can end in separation or divorce. In fact, many divorced couples testify that money management problems were a major factor in the dissolution of their marriage.

Probably no mature American needs to be told that debt is bad. It is almost like telling someone who smokes that it is harmful. The person already knows that. What he or she needs is some help in overcoming the smoking habit. I believe the counsel in this chapter will assist anyone who desires to be debt-free.

When it finally dawns on us that God owns everything and that we are simply stewards of our possessions, it really puts debt in a new light. For example, we know that all things being equal, we should seek the security of home ownership. However, does that counsel include a 30-year mortgage? I don't think so. I am beginning to see that the devil uses debt to tie us up so that we can't respond to God's calls for service and/or financial support. Statistics show that a little more than one fourth of church members contribute no tithe or offerings. Does this mean that they are unaffected by calls for financial support for opportunities where doors are wide open to the gospel message?

Impact of Debt

I believe that they don't respond for one of three reasons. First, though some would really like to help, they are so far in debt that they simply cannot afford to get involved. Second, primarily as a matter of ignorance, they do not understand the role that God asks them to play as channels of God's blessings instead of reservoirs for their own pleasure. And third, some have never let the power of God transform them from the natural trait of selfishness to the born-again trait of sacrifice and liberality. It is my sincere prayer and desire that the insights shared in this book will motivate readers to arrange their lifestyles to include a spiritual commitment in the area of finance and debt-free living.

Debt is a particular burden to young couples just beginning life together. It is relatively easy to get a credit card and to "establish credit." So many "necessities" are available on the "easy payment plan." Take a look at the Sunday paper, and you will note that many car companies advertise automobiles by announcing the monthly payment and not the total cost of the car or the duration of the payments.

I counseled with one couple who were $32,000 in debt just on their Visa cards. They were at the point of bankruptcy because of the 19 percent interest on top of their other heavy obligations. How did it happen? It was quite simple, actually. They had Visa accounts and cards from three different banks, each with a $10,000 credit line. The husband used one card (initially to keep travel expenses connected with his work separate from family expenses). In addition, the wife had two Visa cards to make family purchases (so she didn't have to carry cash around all the time, would have records of their expenses, could have a 30-day use of the money without paying interest, and could take advantage of special sales when they didn't have the cash).

By now you probably know what happened to them. First the husband began using the card for personal use while traveling, and then could not pay off the balance with his expense budget. He still had to keep working, of course, so he added more business expenses. Soon interest was accumulating because he no longer could pay off the balance in full each month. Over a period of time he reached his credit limit of $10,000. Meanwhile, the wife had used her cards to the point that not only could she not pay off her balance each month, but she was having to get a cash advance from one card to pay the minimum balance on the other. Soon she was out of control, with both cards maxed out and even beyond her two-card credit limit of $20,000.

Bankruptcy

Another woman who came to me had already been counseled by another attorney that her only alternative was to declare bankruptcy. Feeling that bankruptcy was not the Christian thing to do, she approached me for a second opinion. She told me that her debt load—brought on by a variety of circumstances—was about to take her under financially. For example, she said that she had just made her monthly payment to Sears for $75 and the check was for interest only! Theoretically, she could have paid Sears $75 per month for the rest of her life and never paid off her balance.

Perhaps this would be a good place to give a brief discussion of bankruptcy. Basically, bankruptcy affords those in debt the opportunity to get creditors off their backs by one of two ways. They can have their debts discharged in court—not because there is a dispute as to their validity, but because of the debtors' complete insolvency or inability to pay—or they can seek court protection from creditors while gaining time to reorganize their finances. Then they will pay back all or a portion of the debts owed over a specified period of time.

Very simply, chapter 7 of the U.S. Bankruptcy Code is a total or complete discharge of debt. This allows the creditors to receive either nothing or a very small percentage of what a debtor owes based on a division of available assets according to a certain order of priority set by the court. On the other hand, chapter 11 or chapter 13 of the code asks the creditors to stand back and be patient while the debtor reorganizes his or her finances and sets up a court-approved system of repayment, generally with little or no interest charges being assessed.

Frankly, from my perspective, bankruptcy is not an alternative for the Christian even though as discussed in an earlier chapter more than 20,000 American families declare bankruptcy every week, including many professing Christians. God's Word indicates that if we incur a debt we are duty-bound before God to pay it. I am sure you can imagine how you would feel if someone who owed you money declared bankruptcy and left you holding the bag financially. You certainly would not consider it a positive Christian witness.

Some with serious debt have little choice as to whether or not they will claim protection under the bankruptcy code. They simply find themselves forced into bankruptcy by their creditors' demands. The law calls this "involuntary bankruptcy." It seems to me that those who face this situation should seek to arrange for a reorganization-type bankruptcy so that they can fairly pay back those who trusted them with the credit.

Just before I share with you a simple plan of how to get out of debt, I want to address a topic that financial or stewardship circles do not often discuss, one that I first learned about while studying with Larry Burkett and Christian Financial Concepts. That topic is surety. One of the first things that probably pops into your head when you hear the word is collateral or cosigning. There one individual becomes surety for another. Both Scripture and Ellen White highly discourage cosigning or becoming surety for another. An example would be Proverbs 6:1-5, which in essence tells us, "If you have become surety for a friend or a stranger, you are caught in a snare. You should do your very best to free yourself. Go humble yourself before your friend and plead with that person to release you. Do not sleep until you are free. Deliver yourself like a gazelle from the hand of the hunter or like a bird from the hand of the trapper."

Dangers of Cosigning

Remember that the banks make their living by lending money. It upsets them when a potential customer does not qualify for a loan. As you are well aware, when anyone gets turned down for a loan, it is because that individual is a poor credit risk. He or she has been a slow payer, has defaulted on a previous loan, lacks the ability to pay, etc. Now the bank says to the high-risk customer, "We would like to help you, but you will need to get someone with established credit to cosign with you." If you cosign for someone, what really happens is that you are getting the loan and must stand good for it, but you give the proceeds of the loan to the high-risk person.

In a high percentage of cases the cosigner ends up paying the loan back. Many times the person cosigned with is a church member or relative. This can cause serious social problems and tensions. (In fact, one definition of a distant relative is one that owes you money!) The bottom line on cosigning is, simply, don't do it!

"Personal Surety"

This brings us to another equally dangerous though little recognized practice—even though it is much more widely practiced. It is called "personal surety." Very simply, it is becoming personally responsible for debts beyond the value of the mortgaged object. An illustration will help you grasp this concept.

Some time ago a woman called me after being involved in an automobile accident. She needed assistance in getting her car replaced and being compensated for the personal injuries sustained by her and her passengers.

Her story is a sad one but repeated daily across the country. The facts in a nutshell are as follows: On a late spring day at the end of the school year she had driven some distance in her Toyota to pick up her daughter for her summer job and time at home with the family. Riding with them was a young man, a classmate of the daughter who was also from the same town. About four miles from the school a man driving a Suburban (a truck-sized station wagon) ran a stop sign and plowed into the side of their car. The impact alone totaled their car, but it also knocked them across the double yellow line of the four-lane road into the path of an 18-wheeler loaded with nearly 40,000 pounds of freight. Fortunately the large truck was stopped as the driver prepared to make a left turn, or all the occupants of the car would have been killed. In any event, the Toyota lodged partway under the big truck, and the front bumper of the truck broke out the front window of the car. Miraculously, all three occupants of the car survived. All were taken to the hospital in separate ambulances. The mother, the driver of the car, had the most serious injuries, and accordingly required the most medical care. The daughter, though injured the least, spent most of her summer break taking care of her mother and keeping house for her. The young man's facial lacerations were so disfiguring that the restaurant that had promised him a summer job now refused to hire him.

All this happened with no fault on the mother's part. The driver of the Suburban assumed all liability. In fact, when the woman called me about one month after the accident, she stated that the insurance company of the other party had already called her twice, offering to pay her the full wholesale value of her car in cash. "I didn't know that you were a car dealer," I replied.

"Oh," she said, "I'm not. Why did you say that?" I explained that she would have to pay retail value to replace her car, so she should ask for retail value for her damaged car. She quickly agreed. After determining from her the make and model of the wrecked vehicle, I checked the NADA automobile price book to determine the value of her car. I had also asked her if she had done anything to enhance its value. She responded that she had just had a new set of tires put on and a complete tune-up before the trip to the school. The total at the auto shop was $300.

The book stated that the retail value of her year-old car was $5,800, to which I added the $300, making a total retail settlement cost of $6,100. I phoned the insurance company of the Suburban owner and explained to the claims adjuster that I was representing the woman who had been hit by his insured motorist. Since there was no question about liability, he quickly told me that he had already called to settle with my client. I told him that I was aware of his offer but that we wanted the full retail value plus the additional value of the tires and tune-up. He quickly replied that his company did not pay for tires or tune-ups, since that was a part of normal wear and tear. To make the story short, I will just tell you that the next day I picked up a check at his office for the full $6,100. I was happy for the good settlement and called my client to share the news.

After I explained to her the settlement amount, she did not answer for a few seconds. When I asked her if there was some problem, she said, "Well, sort of. I owe $9,100 on the car." The accident was not her fault, but although she received full retail value for the car, she still came up $3,000 short of the payoff. What were her options now? Would Toyota Motor Credit take the $6,100 as the full payoff for the car? No, as a matter of fact they billed her for the $3,000 difference, and she had to pay it from the proceeds of her medical settlement. The $3,000 difference between what she owed on the car and its retail value is "personal surety." It is what you are personally responsible for beyond the value of the collateral.

A sad fact is that the vast majority of those purchasing automobiles on the monthly payment plan owe far more on their cars than they are worth because of two reasons. First is the low down payment required to purchase a car in today's competitive market. Frequently a purchaser can buy a new car with no out-of-pocket expense. He can use the "rebate" for his down payment and finance the balance over five years for a total of 60 payments. And this brings me to the second major problem. The fact is that for most cars, depreciation during the first two years wipes out about 50 percent of their original value. Accordingly, if you make either no or a low down payment, then almost from the first day the purchaser is "upside down" in the loan.

Auto Financing Scam

While I am on the subject of cars, I should alert you to the following auto financing scam that is actually legal in some states. In Tennessee, for example, it is legal for the lending institution to charge you all the interest that you would have paid over the life of your automobile loan no matter when you pay it off! In the past it was generally understood that if because of hard work or some good fortune you came up with some extra money, you could call your lending institution and ask, "What is my payoff?" The lender would give you a payoff figure that was your "principal" balance on the loan, thereby allowing you to save the interest you would have paid if you had allowed the loan to go to term. Under the new law the company can just say, "Tear out all the remaining coupons in your payment book, add them up, and that is your payoff." As I stated before, you pay all the interest no matter when you pay off the loan. To avoid such prepayment penalties, carefully read your loan agreement papers before you sign anything.

Remember that personal surety is the difference between what you owe and the value of your collateral. Consider this situation. For several years I have carried an American Express travel card. One reason is that American Express requires cardholders to pay off their balance at the end of each month. In addition, it is handy to guarantee late arrival for a hotel room or for getting a rental car. One day I received a letter in the mail from American Express Privileged Access Line. The letter stated in part, "I am pleased to enclose your personal application for an extraordinary line of credit of up to $100,000, requiring absolutely no collateral." The no-collateral part was underlined. When I read this I said to Kathy, "Wow, what we couldn't do with $100,000."

"We couldn't pay it back, that's what we couldn't do," she instantly replied. And she was right. But what really got me thinking was the part about no collateral. If a loan does not require a specific collateral and you sign the agreement, what is the collateral? What is the security for the lending institution? It is everything you presently own plus whatever else is necessary to pay off the loan from your future earnings. This is 100 percent personal surety!

Why is debt so bad? Well, in addition to the pressure and stress of financial bondage that causes untold problems in the marriage and family arena, you have the added problem of so much of your money being siphoned off to pay interest. Consider this statement:

"There are only two places in the world where we can deposit our treasures—in God's storehouse or in Satan's, and all that is not devoted to Christ's service is counted on Satan's side and goes to strengthen his cause" (*Testimonies,* vol. 6, p. 448).

With this thought in mind, remember what happens when a family buys a home with a 30-year mortgage. For a $100,000 loan at 12 percent, the total payoff is more than $300,000. That means that you will pay more than $200,000 in interest. How much of the $200,000 interest helps to advance the cause of God? The answer is: none! No self-respecting Christian would ever sit down and write a check to the devil, but when we are in debt he effectively siphons off large portions of our income (the interest we pay) so that these funds can never be used to advance God's cause. Those in debt find that it takes all that they can earn just to keep their heads above water. Consequently they have little or nothing left to help others or the church, the only ways to store up treasure in heaven (*ibid.,* vol. 2, p. 279; vol. 3, p. 546).

Before I suggest a solution to the debt problem, let me share just briefly the basic counsel regarding debt from Ellen White (who echoes that of the Bible). "Many, very many, have not so educated themselves that they can keep their expenditures within the limit of their income. . . . They borrow and borrow again and again and become overwhelmed in debt, and consequently they become discouraged and disheartened" (*The Adventist Home,* p. 374).

Sadly, a Seventh-day Adventist can go all the way through our school system—first grade through college—and never have to take a course in which he or she learns how to manage personal finances. This is true even though each and every person will face such decisions throughout life. Also the vast majority of failed marriages have financial problems as one of the major reasons for their breakup.

Debt Is Slavery

The Bible says, "The rich rules over the poor, and the borrower is servant [slave] to the lender" (Proverbs 22:7). A tongue-in-cheek definition of the golden rule is that the one who has the gold makes the rules. A good illustration of this happened just recently when a woman and her college-aged daughter asked to speak with me after one of my public seminars. She told how two years before, her daughter had taken out a student loan to assist her through school. The next year she stayed out of school to work and save up money. During her year out she overpaid her taxes by $530. Dutifully filling out her IRS form 1040EZ, she sent it in, showing her expected tax return of $530. In a few weeks she received an envelope from the IRS that she assumed would contain her tax return check. Instead it had a letter that stated that she had figured her taxes correctly, and that they had applied the money to her student loan. The borrower is the slave of the lender.

While writing to a man in debt, Ellen White said, "This has been the curse of your life, getting into debt. Avoid it as you would the smallpox" (*ibid.,* p. 393).

In Ellen White's day one of the worst diseases you could get was smallpox. If you did come down with it, the prognosis was almost always death. What disease would she have compared debt to today? AIDS? The point is, we should avoid debt like the plague it is.

The apostle Paul counseled, "Let no debt remain outstanding, except the continuing debt to love one another" (Romans 13:8, NIV).

Whose idea was debt, anyway? Why is it such a national scourge at every level—personal, corporate, government? Every society has always had at least a small percentage who, because of mismanagement, unfortunate circumstances, etc., have been poor and therefore somewhat indebted to society. But today it seems that almost everyone is in debt. I believe that Satan inspired such a high level of debt to tie up God's people and hinder the cause of God as a result. "When one becomes involved in debt, he is in one of Satan's nets, which he sets for souls. . . . Deny yourself a thousand things rather than run into debt" (*ibid.,* pp. 392, 393).

How to Eliminate Debt

Surely by now you realize that debt is bad. Now comes the good news. I believe that it is possible for almost any family, if they really want to get out of debt (with the exception of their home mortgage, which we will discuss in chapter 8), to do so within 18 months to two years. I will now outline the plan that has worked for us and has helped scores of other families eliminate their consumer debt.

The plan is simple. It has a basic premise and three steps. The steps all come from *Counsels on Stewardship,* page 257 (originally written in 1877).

This debt elimination model rests on the assumption that the person following it has made a commitment to faithful tithing, thus accessing God's wisdom and blessing (see Proverbs 3; Deuteronomy 28; Malachi 3; Matthew 6; and Matthew 25).

Step 1:
Declare a moratorium on additional debt.
- No more credit spending.
- If you don't borrow money, you can't get into debt.
- If you don't borrow any more money, you can't get further into debt.

Step 2:
Make a covenant with God that from this point on, as He blesses, you will pay off your debts as quickly as possible.
Set a target date for being debt-free. When God blesses you financially, use it to reduce debt—not to purchase more things.

This step is probably the most critical. The reason is that when most people acquire unexpected money, they simply spend it. They will "splurge" or use it as a down payment on another purchase and thereby go even further into debt. One man deeply in debt I talked with received some money and said, "How did God know that I needed a new riding lawn mower?" If you have made the covenant (promise or agreement) with God, then you will know what to do with the extra money. You will apply it to your debt-reduction plan.

Step 3:
Make a list of all your debts from the largest to the smallest in descending order, as in the illustration below.

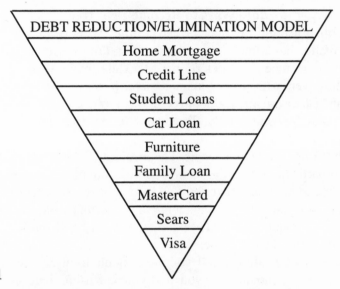

DEBT REDUCTION/ELIMINATION MODEL
Home Mortgage
Credit Line
Student Loans
Car Loan
Furniture
Family Loan
MasterCard
Sears
Visa

Figure 1

Begin by making at least the minimum payment due on each of your debts on a monthly basis. Next, double up or increase in any way you can your payments on the debt on the bottom of the list. You will be happily surprised how quickly you can eliminate that smallest debt. Then use the money that you were paying on the bottom debt to add to the basic payment on the debt listed next. As you eliminate your smaller high-interest debts, you will free up a surprising amount of money to place on the next level.

By starting at the bottom of the list, you will have many occasions to praise God for His blessings and for the freedom you are beginning to experience.

When you reach the home mortgage debt at the top of the list, you will be able to employ the money that you once spent on consumer debt to make regular additional principal payments, thereby reducing the length of your home loan by several months or even years. We will go into more detail on the home mortgage payoff in chapter 8.

By following these three simple steps, many families have become debt- free. You can too! By putting God first, you will receive His wisdom and blessing for managing what He has entrusted to you.

In closing this chapter, I want to underscore my firm belief that once you put this plan into practice, you will see God's hand in your release from financial bondage. In addition, I will now share with you some things that you can do to provide extra cash to speed up step 3. Use as many of the following ideas as you can.

More Ways to Become Debt-free

• Establish a family budget. Most families will spend whatever they make no matter how much they earn. Once a family has put a budget in place, then its members can determine if they are living within their means or not. Moreover, with proper management, it is possible to know when surplus funds are available for debt-reduction purposes.

• Set goals for your family. Treat your family finances as a business. Make rational decisions regarding your expenditures, savings, investments, etc. Establish debt-reduction goals. Determine that by a certain date you will have a particular bill or debt paid off. For example, if you owe on your car, set a date in the future that you will have it paid off. Naturally it should be earlier than when your last payment would normally have fallen. If you have more cars than you really need, you could sell one and use the proceeds to pay on the other one.

• Destroy your credit cards if you are not able to discipline yourself to pay them off every month or if you find yourself using them to buy items that would not be a part of your regular budget.

• Purchase depreciating items with cash. In some localities the local supermarkets accept credit cards for food. You actually eat the food before the bill comes in the mail.

• Begin economy measures. You have heard this routine many times before, but the list of items here is almost endless. Cut down on the length and/or frequency of long-distance phone calls. Don't go grocery shopping when you are hungry. Save electricity when you can. Carpool. Don't eat out as often.

• Have a sale. Most people have hundreds of dollars' worth of "junk" or "stuff" that they have accumulated for years and will never use again. Have a yard sale. Sell big ticket items that you really are not using to good advantage, such as vacation homes, recreational vehicles, airplanes, motorcycles, boats, etc.

Even if you don't need to sell these items to become debt-free, why not liquidate them anyway to help advance the cause of God while the objects are still worth something, while we can still spend money to further the mission of the church. As we approach the end of time we should cut the cords that bind us to this earth so that when Jesus comes the fires at the end will not burn up much of our stuff (see *Counsels on Stewardship,* p. 60).

Some of these things are easier said than done. The debt-reduction plan and the family budget will work, but you may have to sacrifice in order to be successful. I believe an illustration from my own family's experience could help explain this.

Many years ago when I was about 14 years old I remember living in a city where there was a small custom boat manufacturing company. It built power boats for skiing and pleasure riding. The craft intrigued me because they used large V-8 engines for the power plants, with direct-drive power shafts. Of course, the boats were very powerful and "pleasant to the eye." Once while visiting the company, I said to myself, "Someday when I get through school and get a good job, I am going to get myself a boat like that." More than 20 years went by. Then one summer day in 1981 during our family's vacation we attended a waterski show in which they used the new powerful competition ski boats constructed by the Mastercraft Company.

As we left the ski show the exit route for obvious reasons took us through the gift and souvenir shop. In the building they had a cutaway cross section of the beautiful Mastercraft boat showing its quality design and its beautifully polished 240-horsepower V-8 engine. While I stood there looking at that display, a little bell went off in my head, and something reminded me, "There is that boat that you promised yourself when you were a kid." About two months later we picked up our boat at the dealership. Later we even bought a Suburban station wagon in a matching color to tow it.

The purchase was a good deal for our family. We all learned to ski and had many fun times together. In addition, we used it for church campouts, ministerial meetings, etc. In the fall of 1988 when we were in high gear in our "debt-reduction mode," Kathy suggested during our evening worship that we could sell the boat to better our financial position and put money in savings for emergency purposes. She went on to say that we had used the boat only twice that year. Besides that, we were paying insurance on it for all year, and it was taking up space in the garage.

I was raised in a very Spartan environment. My parents worked hard so that we could attend church school. Thus we had no money for summer camp or other optional things. Mom and Dad never owned their own home, had a new set of furniture, or bought a new car. I am telling you this so that you can partly understand that whether or not we ever used the boat again, the fact that we had it was enough satisfaction for me.

Fortunately, Kathy suggested the possibility of selling the boat in October when the ski season for the year was past. Accordingly, I felt that there probably wouldn't be much of a market for a ski boat at that time of year. So instead of saying, "No way, we are not selling the boat; don't even mention it," I replied, "Well, that may be something to consider. Why don't we advertise the boat for 90 percent of what we paid for it, and if it is God's will that we sell it, someone will buy it." Naturally I hoped that it wouldn't sell and that by spring we would all be excited about skiing again. In addition, though we had kept the boat in immaculate condition, it did have eight skiing seasons' worth of use. And of course, usually a boat is a highly depreciating item, and people usually aren't willing to pay that much for so old a craft. Well, to make a long story short, we advertised the boat, and the first person that looked at it paid cash for it.

I believe many of you will be able to understand how I felt when the purchaser hooked our boat to his car and towed it away. Part of me went with it. I still miss it! But then I remember that soon we will all have to walk off and leave all our earthly possessions. How much easier it will be if we have liquidated much of them before that day. Now I understand why Jesus said in Luke 17:32 in the context of getting ready for His second coming, "Remember Lot's wife."

APPLICATION
Chapter 5

1. Take the time to list all of your outstanding debts in descending order from the largest to the smallest.

2. Make a covenant with God that as He blesses, you will use the money to reduce your debts. If you wish, you could put this in writing in your prayer list and sign it.

3. Develop your debt-reduction/payoff strategy. Establish a faithful tithe and live prudently.

4. Arrange to liquidate any of your possessions that you can live without to assist in the debt-reduction process.

◆

CHAPTER SIX

"Through wisdom a house is built, and by understanding it is established; by knowledge the rooms are filled with all precious and pleasant riches" (Proverbs 24:3, 4).

Budgeting Suggestions

I have made it a practice over the past few years to ask those who come to me for counseling the same opening question. After we have exchanged pleasantries and introduced ourselves, I ask, "What do you perceive your problem to be?" Most of the time the answer is the same: "We don't make enough money." Some earning three or four times what I receive still give the same answer. At a party several young couples were discussing the difficulties of family budgets. "I really don't want a lot of money," said one yuppie. "I just wish we could afford to live the way we're living now."

40 Percent Overspend Every Month

How typical this sentiment is. In fact, a study conducted by the Christian Financial Concepts organization discovered that, in a sampling of 6,000 Christian families, 40 percent overspend every month. That means they pay out more than they make—something possible only because of the availability of credit and debt. The study pointed out two other significant factors. An equal percentage—40 percent—pay at least $2,000 per year in consumer interest (excluding mortgages). Of course, such interest is no longer tax-deductible. The sad fact is that such financial difficulties have had a serious adverse effect on the stability of the Christian family. Today Christians have the same divorce statistics as the general population. Fifty percent of all marriages end in divorce. But here is the most significant factor. Ninety percent of those who divorce point to financial difficulties as the major factor in the breakup of their marriage.

If we can help our families to manage and control their finances properly, we can save a lot of marriages and thus strengthen our homes and ultimately the church.

Probably the major culprit in the financial crisis facing most families is not the amount of money that they make, but rather their ignorance of how to handle or manage it, combined with poor planning habits. This includes for many couples the failure to establish a budget and to live within it. In fact, it appears to me that many families have no plan at all. They just live from paycheck to paycheck and pay the creditor that screams the loudest.

In this chapter I will outline for you what I consider to be a simple method of money management that allows you to create your own budget and thereby live within your means. I believe that each family's needs, though similar, are unique, and therefore, just as with will and estate planning documents, each budget must be tailor-made. But we can all look at the major expenditures that a typical family makes and then adjust our budget to meet our individual needs.

The problems begin when a couple says, "We make a reasonable income, but we don't know where the money goes." Another common phenomenon today is that the average family will spend whatever they make no matter how much it is. So what I will urge in this chapter is that each family develop a reasonable lifestyle that utilizes the biblical principal of contentment (see Hebrews 13:5 and 1 Timothy 6:6ff.) and determine by the use of a simple budget how much is enough for family needs.

When we read verses like Malachi 3:10, it seems clear that God wants us to have more than we need. He says, "I will . . . open for you the windows of heaven and pour out for you such blessing that there will not be room enough to receive it." Now, if you don't have room enough for it, you have a surplus. How much would God have to give your family before you would say, "We now have enough. God must be wanting us to share this with others"? We will never know enough unless we follow a budget and recognize what our true needs really are.

"Money has great value, because it can do great good. . . . But money is of no more value than sand, only as it is put to use in providing for the necessities of life, in blessing others, and advancing the cause of Christ" (*Christ's Object Lessons,* p. 351). God always blesses us first. And then it is from the surplus beyond our needs that He asks us to help others and to contribute to His cause.

Without a budget, money leaks through our hands like water from a dripping faucet. And like water, too much of our income goes down the drain. It is the uncontrolled dripping that causes the loss. A faucet that drips only one drop per second will waste 200 gallons of water in one month! In the same way, uncontrolled and unaccounted-for money adds up to a substantial sum and a drain on the family economy. The very best way to control your money and get the most out of it is through the use of a budget.

If you are married, both you and your spouse should work together to develop and maintain your family budget. I recommend that you spend several hours together initially to set up the budget and then take the steps necessary to modify your spending habits to fit it. One of the basic tools to getting a control on spending and living on a budget is your checking account. We use a checkbook with a carbon copy backup so we will never forget what we wrote a check for or what the amount was. In addition, that way we always know where our money went. Kathy has the greatest interest in detail work in our family and is willing to keep the checkbook balanced and arrange for our agreed-upon expenditures. So when we get our regular income we deposit it immediately into our interest-bearing checking account so that no money slips through the cracks. Usually we keep out a small amount of money—about $20 per month each—that we do not have to give an account for, but that is it.

Sample Budget

Now let's look at a sample budget. With permission from Larry Burkett and Christian Financial Concepts, I have used the guideline budget that they have developed, because of its simplicity and adaptability. Most budgets that I have seen over the years either leave out God altogether or are so complex that no one but a family of nerds would take the time to follow it.

The basic budget (Figure 2) is entitled "A Short-Range Plan." It is designed to enable you to see the overall picture of your spending needs and habits. The second page of the budget (Figure 3) covers "monthly income and expenses." With these two pages you can quickly figure out both where you are and where you ought to be financially. I suggest that you photocopy the two pages so that you can begin to formulate your own customized budget plan.

While this budget is not fleshed out in full detail and leaves out some important items like Christian education expenses, which I will address later in this chapter, the basic principles outlined here are sound and will assist you to develop your own plan. It is the basic budget that we follow and that we use in our seminars.

Let's take an overview of the guideline budget. First, notice that it has three distinct categories. They are: *Income*—from all sources; *nondiscretionary expenses*—tithe (and systematic offerings) and taxes (federal, state, and FICA); and n*et spendable income*—the source from which we develop the budget.

Income

Since more detail is necessary to see the big picture, I will go over these three items again. Your *income* is the heart of your budget because you can't spend more than you make. So whatever you earn is what you

A SHORT-RANGE PLAN

Guidelines for a Family of Four

	Income $15,000	Income $30,000	My Income $ _____
Tithe	10%	12%	_____%
Taxes (federal, state, FICA)	18%	21%	_____%
	28%	33%	_____%
	72% ($10,800)	67% ($20,100)	____%(____)
Net Spendable Income	$10,800 ÷ 12 = $900 month	$20,100 ÷ 12 = $1,675 month	$ _____ ÷ 12 = $ ____month
Housing	35% ($315)	30% ($503)	____%(____)
Food	17% ($153)	15% ($251)	____%(____)
Auto	17% ($153)	17% ($285)	____%(____)
Insurance	3% ($ 27)	5% ($ 84)	____%(____)
Debts	5% ($ 45)	5% ($ 84)	____%(____)
Entertainment/ Recreation	5% ($ 45)	5% ($ 84)	____%(____)
Clothing	5% ($ 45)	5% ($ 84)	____%(____)
Savings	5% ($ 45)	10% ($168)	____%(____)
Medical/Dental	3% ($ 27)	3% ($ 50)	____%(____)
Miscellaneous	5% ($ 45)	5% ($ 84)	____%(____)

Note: These figures are only guidelines, not imperatives. However, a budget that is far different from the one above is probably unbalanced and reflects wrong priorities. The tax and tithe may be different from the examples shown, but the important figure in this illustration is net spendable income, since the percentages are all based on that amount.

MONTHLY INCOME AND EXPENSES

INCOME PER MONTH	_____	**7. Debts**	_____
Salary	_____	Credit card	_____
Interest	_____	Loans, notes	_____
Dividends	_____	Other	_____
Notes	_____	**8. Entertainment and Recreation**	_____
Rents	_____	Eating out	_____
		Trips	_____
TOTAL GROSS INCOME	_____	Baby-sitters	_____
		Activities	_____
LESS:		Vacation	_____
1. Tithe	_____	Other	_____
2. Tax	_____	**9. Clothing**	_____
NET SPENDABLE INCOME	═══		
		10. Savings	_____
3. Housing	_____		
Mortgage (rent)	_____	**11. Medical**	_____
Insurance	_____	Doctor	_____
Taxes	_____	Dentist	_____
Electricity	_____	Drugs	_____
Gas	_____	Other	_____
Water	_____		
Sanitation	_____	**12. Miscellaneous**	_____
Telephone	_____	Toiletry, cosmetics	_____
Maintenance	_____	Beauty, barber	_____
Other	_____	Laundry, cleaning	_____
		Allowances, lunches	_____
4. Food	_____	Subscriptions	_____
		Gifts (incl. Christmas)	_____
5. Automobile(s)	_____	Special education	_____
Payments	_____	Cash	_____
Gas and oil	_____	Other	_____
Insurance	_____		
License/registration	_____	**TOTAL EXPENSES**	═══
Taxes	_____		
Maintenance/repair/		**INCOME VS. EXPENSE**	
replacement	_____	**Net Spendable Income**	_____
		Less Expenses	_____
6. Insurance	_____		
Life	_____		═══
Medical	_____		
Other	_____		

Figure 3

(From "Your Finances in Changing Times," by Larry Burkett. Copyright 1990, Christian Financial Concepts, Inc. Used with permission.)

IYM-3

must base your budget and standard of living upon. The best budget ideas seek to maximize income and minimize expenses. Obviously, the more income you have, the more flexibility you will have in the budgeting process. As I mentioned earlier in this chapter, most people feel that they just don't earn enough when many times the real problem is proper management.

Some families feel that if the wife would go to work it would solve their financial problems. She will bring in significant additional income only if she is a trained professional. Her working will create additional expenses, such as tithe, taxes, Social Security, transportation, food away from home, extra for clothes and cleaning, child care, gifts for fellow workers, etc.—and can in some cases actually cost more than the income!

If your income is not regular, such as that of a commissioned salesperson, you must estimate your monthly income based on last year's income. A self-employed person must take into account all required taxes and annual self-employment Social Security payments when computing net income.

Nondiscretionary Expense

The *nondiscretionary expense* is the next category in the budgeting process. For the Christian, tithe is really nondiscretionary. In other words, one does not decide whether or not he or she can afford to tithe. When you accept God and His word, you place His requirements first and allow Him to bless the balance. The tithe is not a tax, but rather God's part of our covenant relation with Him, as we discussed in chapter 4. It appears in the nondiscretionary category only because of its special significance. Taxes are also a nondiscretionary expense. If we have income beyond a certain level, we have tax consequences. It's just that simple.

Net Spendable Income

The last category is the *net spendable income* section. Once you have determined your income and subtracted from it your tithe (and systematic offerings) and taxes, then the balance becomes the amount upon which you base your budget. This net spendable income becomes 100 percent of what you have to spend. Then you divide that 100 percent into the 10 major categories by percentages that add up to 100 percent. This budget is quite flexible and serves only as a guide for the average family's spending habits. You may adjust the percentages as necessary to meet your particular lifestyle, but in no case can your percentages equal more than 100 percent, or you will be going into debt.

From a Christian perspective, a family should try to minimize their own needs and therefore lower the percentages required in each given category if possible, so as to be able to help others and God's cause. I will address this more in chapter 12. Having said all this, I realize it is still true that many families will find that they are not able even to fit into this budget, let alone have a surplus to share. So let's go to work after we look at the "Monthly Income and Expenses" of the budget and discuss ways to conserve.

The figure entitled "Monthly Income and Expenses" helps us actually to "put the numbers to our financial spending habits." Note that it is just an expansion of the guideline budget. Again we find three major categories. First there is income, which includes everything you earn, whether you receive it weekly, biweekly, monthly, quarterly, or annually. These funds are then converted to monthly amounts. The second category contains the nondiscretionary uses or expenditures. And finally, that amount of money left after tithe (and offerings here, if you choose) and taxes is the net spendable income, upon which the budget is based.

The guideline budget contains 10 major categories or sections into which you divide the net spendable income. For purposes of the budget the net spendable income is 100 percent of the available money. The 10 sections each receive a percentage of the total as the individual family's needs dictate. The percentages given to each category can vary greatly between families, but in no case can a family spend more than a total of 100 percent or they will wind up in debt.

Perhaps it would be a good idea to photocopy the monthly income and expenses page and do some simple calculations to see how you are presently doing. First determine the total monthly income available to your family. Second, deduct your tithe and taxes to figure out your net spendable income. At this point you are ready to fill in your monthly spending habits in the 10 sections of the NSI. Then add up your actual expenditures and compare this total with your monthly income. If you are making more than you are spending, you may stop and rejoice before going further in the book. You are in the enviable position of having a surplus. Funds that you can use to store up money in heaven by helping others and God's work. I will explain this concept more in chapter 12.

If you find, as we did when we first tried to fill out this form, that you are spending more each month than you make, then you must take a good look at each section to see where you are higher than the suggested percentage and make corrections if you can. Even if you have a surplus, it is good to examine each section to see if you can improve your stewardship. Let's take a look at each section and see what improvements we can suggest.

Housing

You will note that the guideline budget suggests spending only about

30 percent of your income for housing. It is interesting to note that many mortgage lending institutions will lend money for a home mortgage with monthly payments up to 30 percent of the monthly income. However, the housing section contains much more than just the house payment or rent. It also includes insurance, property taxes, utilities (electricity, gas, water, and sanitation), telephone, maintenance, and other costs, such as association fees. Just from the housing section alone it is easy to see how difficult it is to buy your own home in today's high-priced housing market. Even if a family makes $30,000 per year and all their other housing expenses, including utilities and telephone, total only $100 per month, that would leave only about $400 per month for rent or house payment. What kind of house would $400 per month buy? Kind of sounds like a you-fix-up starter home to me. But remember, you can borrow a few percentages from other sections if you can get by with a smaller amount there.

We have all read books or articles about saving money on utility bills by implementing energy-saving features. You can also cut way down on the long-distance phone bill by calling during the least expensive times and limiting the length.

Food

Depending upon where you live, you may or may not be able to cut down on your food bill. If you have the space to develop a vegetable garden, you will find that one will offer you several advantages. For example, there are the vine-ripened tomatoes and other bounties from the garden that you can eat fresh and/or preserve for later use. Then consider the physical exercise so greatly needed by modern families.

Eating out socially on an occasional basis should come under the category of entertainment and recreation. When home economists study food costs, they discover that when a family eats only one meal a day out, it adds to the amount spent on food in a dramatic way. Let me illustrate this point. A family that I know personally lived in the community of one of our schools. The parents were both teachers and the children both attended as students. Instead of packing a lunch at home and bringing it to school each day, the family chose to eat in the school cafeteria. At the time the school charged $3 per meal. Now when you multiply the four people times $3 per meal that equals $12 per day. Then multiply the $12 times the 21 working/school days per month, and you have the amazing total of $252 dollars per month. It is easy to see that eating out just one meal a day can effectively double the food budget per month! Incidentally, a Department of Agriculture study found that it costs about 80 percent more to have a comparable meal at a fast-food restaurant than at home.

Other well-known pointers pertaining to the food budget apply here.

Prepare a menu for the week and shop only for the ingredients you are going to need for the menu. Don't go grocery shopping when you are hungry or have hungry companions. And one final point—review your household eating and drinking habits. Junk food and soft drinks are expensive and damaging to your health. Either totally eliminate or greatly reduce such items.

Automobile(s)

One of the major expenditures after housing in the typical American family budget is transportation. For most families, transportation includes owning one or more vehicles. When you look at the guideline budget, you can see that it recommends only $285 for auto expenses on an income of $30,000. What kind of car can you buy for that amount? Not a very fancy one, for sure. It becomes even more apparent that you must exercise prudence in this category when you consider that it also includes not just the monthly car payments, but also gas and oil, insurance, license and inspection fees, taxes, repair and maintenance, and saving for a replacement car!

What can be done to reduce costs in this area? Again, whole books have been written on this subject, but I will list a few tips here. First of all, when choosing a car, it is important to keep economy in mind, not only in the initial purchase, but also in the operating costs. In other words, make sure that you purchase your economy car at a good price. Some find good deals by buying year-old cars from auto rental companies such as Hertz or Avis. In so doing, they can save the high first-year depreciation costs and still get a car with most of the manufacturer's warranty still in effect.

Other auto expense cost-saving items include reducing the use of your automobile. Carpool whenever possible. Consolidate your trips to town. Walk or bike more. A study done by Hertz concluded that the cost of owning and operating a typical new compact car driven for 10,000 miles per year for five years was 47 cents a mile. The less you drive, the less you spend.

Many families discover that they can save a considerable amount by learning to do simple automobile repair and maintenance. If you don't know how, watch the paper for adult education classes provided by local schools. You will soon find that you know more about your particular car than some of the unskilled "mechanics" that you will encounter.

Insurance

This is an area of real concern to me. Many families don't seem to realize that one cannot insure against every eventuality. Good, basic coverage is all that most need. In my opinion, you should not think of insurance as an investment, but rather for what it is supposed to be—

coverage for your debts and other expenses should you die and leave someone dependent on your income. When you are in debt and your children are small, you may feel that you need insurance. If you do get some, I suggest term insurance. The premiums are about 75 percent cheaper for the same coverage. Purchasing level premium and constant policy amount term insurance will protect you during the time you are paying on your house and/or your children are still home and in school.

Personally, I don't recommend spending large portions of your hard-earned money for life insurance premiums. The company is betting you won't need it for a long time, while you are thinking that you never know what might happen. The company is usually right, and gets the best benefit from the bargain. In addition, like the savings and loan institutions and the banks, insurance companies are beginning to fail. Remember Executive Life in California? Because of bad investments, changes in the economy, graft and corruption in management, and the large settlements paid out of reserves to cover the casualty losses from major natural disasters, many insurance companies are in serious trouble. The insurance industry itself predicts that within the next 10 years the number of viable life insurance companies will drop from the present number of nearly 200 to around 10 solid companies. Many smaller companies will get absorbed by larger ones, but for those who have made bad investments or for any reason just go bankrupt, their clients will face real problems. Who insures the insurance companies? No one. That's right. If your company goes out of business without being picked up by a more solid company, what happens to all the money that you have "invested" in whole life insurance or an annuity? You lose it! It is simply gone.

As for medical insurance, again you must do some study to make sure that you are getting the best deal on the coverage you need. Generally the most economical medical insurance is group insurance offered to a company for its employees and their families. Health-care costs have literally skyrocketed during the past few years. Something must be done about this whole area, but in the meantime you must do your best to pay only for what you actually need while maintaining good health habits. That means a good wholesome vegetarian diet, regular exercise, maintaining your ideal weight, no alcohol or tobacco, and having a positive attitude coupled with trust in God.

Debts

The debt category includes everything other than home mortgage and auto loans as they fall under separate categories. This area does include credit card balances, signature loans, student loans, bill consolidation loans, notes, loans from friends or relatives, etc. If a family can eliminate this debt area, then they can use that percentage of their budget for other categories and at the same time escape the constant pressure from creditors. We discussed a simple and workable debt reduction method in the previous chapter.

Entertainment and Recreation

This category gets left out of most budgets, and many mistakenly feel that they just don't have enough money to fund it. However, inevitably people spend money on it. We eat out, travel for the weekend, hire a baby-sitter, or engage in golf, boating, etc. And of course, if you take a vacation the money must come from somewhere. Without money in this category, many families fund their vacations on their credit cards. It then becomes a debt and has interest added to it. Some suggestions to minimize expense in this area include enjoying the simple pleasures. Cultivate inexpensive hobbies and pleasures—things that can include the whole family. Outdoor activities such as picnicking, hiking, camping. Many find that reading, writing, and visiting with friends and family are excellent alternatives to television and more relaxing, too.

The pet food industry estimated several years ago that, on average, Americans spend more than $40 million a year on dog and cat food. Think how much good that amount could do for the homeless and less fortunate. But closer to home, what about the family budget? All pets cost money. If you pay a lot for them to start with, then you feel obligated to take them to the vet when they are sick or injured. The list of expenditures could go on and on. I once counseled a single-parent woman who was barely making ends meet but had two horses. She had failed to realize how much of her income it took to keep them up until she set up her budget. Why not limit your pets to those your family really enjoys and your budget can afford?

Clothing

Many having trouble making ends meet leave clothing out of their "mental budget" entirely. Or when they make a budget and realize that they are spending more than they make, they decide to drop the clothing category so that they can use the money in other areas. It is true, however, that in Western civilized society we must all appear in public fully clothed. Somehow we always manage to comply with this obligation. The clothes come from somewhere, so we must include them in our budget.

Suggestions to economize in this area are quite fundamental. A man can select one or two basic colors that will look good on him. Then he can change his wardrobe by using a variety of accents such as shirts and ties. You can save money by purchasing traditional fashions in basic colors. Another suggestion is to make a written list of yearly clothing needs for the family. Purchasing clothes from the list during the "off season" will save a considerable amount.

Several budget-conscious families that we know swap children's clothes with friends and relatives. One mother had a standing order with Kathy to purchase at used prices any of Melissa's clothes suitable for her somewhat younger daughter.

Savings

Many families have no savings at all. They just live from paycheck to paycheck with no cushion for emergencies. It is a well-known maxim in personal finance that the truly successful family who has the discipline to live on a budget also has a reasonable liquid savings account. It means that they have money readily available for emergency use. Such items could include your refrigerator conking out or the transmission going out of your car.

How much should you have in this account? Generally experts advise an equivalent of three to six months of salary. This means that if you make $2,500 per month, your emergency savings account should contain between $7,500 and $15,000. I know that sounds like a tremendous amount if you presently do not even have a savings account. However, adequate savings is important to keep some unexpected expenditure from "busting your budget." Both the Bible and Ellen White recommend regular savings. In *The Adventist Home* Ellen White suggests that such savings should be used only in an emergency or to make contributions to the church.

What about saving when you are in debt? I suggest that you start saving as a habit immediately, even if it is only a small amount each pay period. It could well be that your present indebtedness resulted from a lack of savings earlier.

Medical

We discussed this topic briefly earlier when talking about health insurance. However, we need to add a little more here. Practice preventive medicine. A healthy family will cost less to maintain. I highly recommend memorizing the acronym for a healthy lifestyle used by Weimar Institute and other health centers—N-E-W S-T-A-R-T. It will allow you to remember the eight natural health laws. They are: proper **nutrition,** regular **exercise**, plenty of **water,** time outdoors in the **sunlight, temperance**— which includes total abstinence from all harmful substances and the moderate use of that which is good—fresh **air,** adequate **rest,** and **trust** in divine power.

Miscellaneous Expenses

This is one of the hardest areas to regulate and control. It becomes a catchall category and never seems to be fully funded to meet all the needs that arise, especially at Christmastime. However, those who have been on a budget for a while find that they are able to bring this area into line as well. A budget gives discipline to spending habits. Imagine how great it would be to have money already set aside for Christmas and other gift-giving occasions.

I hope this brief overview of tips on how to economize will help you. Obviously others have written entire books on just what this chapter covers. I would recommend that you follow the suggestions contained in this chapter and then if you need additional help, you can purchase a copy of Larry Burkett's workbook entitled *How to Manage Your Money*.

There remains one vital topic to discuss that is not a part of the budget outline given at the beginning of this chapter. It is a major category for those families with school-aged children. I am speaking, of course, about Christian education. If your net spendable income is already divided among the 10 major categories listed above, how does a family pay for the cost of Christian education in private schools? The answer for many families is simple and harsh—you sacrifice. I well remember my mother going to work as a nurse's aide so that our family could afford to send the four boys to church school.

Since the budget I have shared in this chapter does not list educational expense, it means that you will have to cut back some of the funded areas during the time the children are in school so that you can use some of their percentage points for schooling. Some families will have to drive the old car a little longer, put off replacing the furniture, avoid going on expensive vacations, or even buying their dream home.

Student Loans

Unfortunately, many families have turned to the student loan program on the college level for assistance with school expenses. I say unfortunately because many students graduate from college owing tremendous amounts of money. In essence, they start out life in debt, sometimes heavy debt. Many couples graduate from college (not medical school) owing $20,000 or $30,000 or more in student loans.

By the way, for most of the regular government guaranteed student loans, the only way that you can get out from under them is to pay it back or die. Even if you file for bankruptcy, you still cannot discharge any taxes you owe, child support payments due, or—you guessed it—student loans. My counsel is: borrow as little as possible.

Financing Christian Education

Well, then, how does a family finance Christian education? I think that you will see that if you look at the counsel in this book as a whole concept or philosophy, things begin to really fit together and make sense. For example, in the next two chapters I will explain how children can work to assist their parents during this time and also how parents can plan to be completely debt-free (including the home mortgage) by the time the children start college so they can offer maximum assistance to them.

When people ask me what I think about student loans, I ask them, "Whatever happened to hard work?" And when I tell them about my own experience of working my way through academy and college, they say, "Well, that isn't possible anymore." Then I suggest that we just brainstorm for a few minutes about the subject and see what we come up with. Here are some of the suggestions we have arrived at:

1. Encourage the students (your children) to recognize that their investment in advanced education is an investment in their future standard of living. Accordingly, their assistance in working summers and during the school year will pay dividends in the future.

2. Parents should plan to be debt-free by the time the kids start college so that they can transfer that large portion of their income that had been used for house payments and put it on educational expenses.

3. Both the parents and the students should be satisfied with prudent living during this time. No expensive new cars for either parents or students unless fully justified in the budget and by necessity.

4. Students, while in academy, should be encouraged to do well academically and prepare properly by using available prep courses for the college entrance exams (SAT and ACT). By so doing, they can become eligible for scholarship grants.

In short, the students can complete college debt-free if they and their parents are willing to work together and live prudently during the college years.

In summary, budgeting is necessary to accomplish your financial goals. If you do not budget, chances are that you are just living from pay period to pay period and on the verge of financial disaster. Budgeting will make your money go further. It is a tool for helping the family meet its needs, get out of debt, and provide for future education and retirement. A budget is also a valuable communication tool for the husband and wife, and as an example for the children to follow in disciplined financial management.

But a budget is useful only if followed. It should be custom-made for your own family's needs. That is why I chose the guideline budget for this book. It is not really a budget, but simply a guide for you to follow in customizing your own. You can adjust it as your income and circumstances change. But keep it simple. Experience tells us that the more complicated a budget, the less likely anyone will keep to it.

Ideally each member of the family should have a small personal allowance to spend freely without having to give an account to one another.

But that is funded from the miscellaneous category and so should include gifts, hobbies, etc.

The key to a successful budget is commitment. A budget is an investment of time that will yield tremendous benefits, including: (1) freedom from unpleasant surprises by keeping you abreast of your financial standing; (2) a surplus to cope with unexpected expenses; (3) the facts necessary to make intelligent financial decisions; and (4) aid in fulfilling your responsibility of becoming a faithful steward. May our Lord richly bless your efforts as you seek to live within your means and budget.

APPLICATION
Chapter 6

1. Carefully list, using your checkbook entries, your receipts, and your memory, your average monthly income and expenses.

2. Now compare your current monthly expenses to the guideline budget.

3. Determine the areas of your budget where you can conserve or make improvement.

4. Decide how much is enough for your family's needs so that you will know when you have a surplus to share with others and make contributions to God.

◆

"And you, fathers, do not provoke your children to wrath, but bring them up in the training and admonition of the Lord" (Ephesians 6:4).

Train Up a Child

In Moses' final speech to the Israelites he charged them, "And these words which I command you today shall be in your heart; you shall teach them diligently to your children and shall talk of them when you sit in your house, when you walk by the way, and when you lie down, and when you rise up" (Deuteronomy 6:6, 7).

We teach children by precept (what we say) and example (what we do). While example is probably the stronger influence, verbal instruction is still important. In this chapter we will consider the practical counsel that we have received about educating children in financial matters.

Obviously, the goal of Christian parents is to raise their children in such a way that they can enter society as independent adults, a goal best accomplished by proper and consistent home training. The media present much today about the breakdown of society, with its resulting problems of crime, violence, underachievement, welfare abuse, etc. We can blame the church, the school, or the government, but when we are really honest with ourselves, the real problem is with the family unit. In some cases it seems that parents give little thought to bringing children into the world and then, once the children come, don't spend much time on their training. However, we as Christians recognize that children are a heritage from the Lord, and we take seriously His counsel to us about their upbringing.

"Every child brought into the world is the property of Jesus Christ, and should be educated by precept and example to love and obey God; but by far the largest number of parents have neglected their God-given work, by failing to educate and train their children, from the first dawning of reason, to know and love Christ. By painstaking effort parents are to watch the opening, receptive mind and make everything in the home life secondary to the positive duty enjoined upon them by God—to train their children in the nurture and admonition of the Lord" (*The Adventist Home*, p. 183).

For young people today the picture is not very bright. The economy is the number one problem today—eclipsing crime, drugs, AIDS, and a host of other problems. Children see that statistically 50 percent of their marriages will fail. Most young couples start out life already in debt as they face car payments, student loans, credit cards, and more. And to compound the problem, they have no financial training. As I mentioned before, it is possible to go all the way through school without learning how to balance a checkbook, buy a car, understand insurance, or discover the best ways of purchasing a home. If you have taught your children these things, they will rise up and call you blessed in the future—and so will their spouses!

Learning to handle money should be a part of every child's education. It is a responsibility that parents should direct themselves and not delegate to teachers, because earning and spending experiences generally take place outside the classroom.

Allowances

One way many parents start their children in their money management training is by providing them an allowance. I believe an allowance should be a relatively small sum, like $2 a week, but given on a regular and systematic basis. From my perspective, an allowance is not something the children "earn," but rather a small sum to allow them to learn the value of money before they are old enough to earn their own. Parents give their children an allowance just because they are members of "our family." With this money children can then learn to tithe and return offerings (giving their own money at church is much more meaningful to children), save for future needs, and spend money for items they wish to purchase.

Paying Your Children

In our family we have practiced a rather old-fashioned concept of "working together" to accomplish family goals. When their respective tenth birthdays arrived, Kathy took Andrew and Melissa downtown to our local bank, which provided no service charge checking accounts for students, and opened an account for them. Since that time they have balanced their own accounts—with assistance at first—and handled their own money on a regular basis.

How did they acquire money to put in their accounts? We had previously discussed this during our worship and family council times, so the children looked forward to the new experience. First we established rules for paying and nonpaying jobs. Each of us as family members performed certain tasks as part of our basic family responsibility. The tasks involved keeping our own rooms clean and tidy, cleaning up after ourselves in the bathroom, helping to set and clear the table, emptying the trash, feeding the pets, etc. However, at age 10 we began to pay our children for more time-intensive jobs. Such as mowing the yard, cleaning the house, washing the cars, keeping our long driveway clean, doing the laundry, cooking for the entire family, and baking bread and preparing granola and special items for Sabbath.

Because during most of this time we were a single-income family, obviously we could not afford a maid or a yard worker. So in exchange we paid the children, and they then took care of their own tuition and purchased most of their own clothing. While these were items that we would have had to pay for anyway, under this arrangement they learned the value and use of money. Our kids had to work at least 20 hours per month just to get enough for their tuition payments. This amounted to about $5.00 per hour, and all went for their elementary school tuition. Then for all that they put in above 20 hours, we paid them $2 an hour. It was from this hourly amount that they made their clothing purchases, started their savings accounts, and obtained their personal spending money.

One important point in the matter of paying children is that once we have agreed to pay them for certain jobs—assuming they perform the work in a satisfactory manner—we were prompt and faithful with the money. Kathy, who is our financial manager, always paid the children for their work right after the tithe and offering checks (which came first, of course) so that we never were short of funds for them. We have followed the practice of making written contracts with our children, signed by them and us, so that there will not be lapses in memory on the part of either party when it comes paytime.

We followed this plan with both of our children from age 10 through graduation from academy. When they entered their academy years they each got summer jobs and worked on the school campus or in town at fast-food establishments. But they always knew that for extra money they could work for us at home.

We have strongly emphasized the value of education for preparation for financial independence. Minimum-wage jobs simply will not support a family budget. Such jobs are primarily to provide work experience for young people entering into the job market and as a supplement to those with other work. Accordingly, our family has always assumed that the children would finish academy and go on to college.

What We Owe Our Children

As I will discuss later in the chapter on estate planning, we have felt, based on our study of the Bible and Ellen White, that we owed our children three things. They are:

1. A Christian home environment. We have attempted to provide a solid religious upbringing. This means regular family worship and church attendance, even participation in church. To us it has also involved practicing Matthew 6:33: "Seek first the kingdom of God and His righteousness, and all these things shall be added to you."

2. A willingness to work and an appreciation for it. Our children learned that money comes to us as a result of our giving time to others by performing tasks valuable to them. They discovered that diligence and integrity at work are always noticed, appreciated, and rewarded. A young person that has never learned to work or manage money is really poorly equipped to enter the job market and live independently.

3. A good education. Education is expensive today—particularly private school education. But to parents with plans for their children not only for this life but for that to come, it is well worth the cost. Frequently during my seminars people ask me what I think about student loans. My first answer is usually "Whatever happened to hard work?" I believe that student loans should be the last resort. The first option should be hard work. In our case we planned for educational expense first of all through prudent living. This means keeping our wants and desires closer to the need level. Then the kids work to the best of their ability during the summers and part-time during the school year, and we their parents also work as hard as we can to supplement their earnings and keep the school statements paid every month. Our goal for each of the children, in lieu of a lump-sum inheritance later, is to assist them to get started in life by making sure that they have no student loans when they graduate and a reasonably good car for transportation. In short, they will have a marketable skill and no debts.

The children can help by doing well in academy so that they are eligible for good student discounts on auto insurance and can qualify for college scholarships.

All the biblical principles for personal money management apply to children as well as adults. Principles like faithfulness in tithing, honesty, diligence, saving for future needs, avoiding debt, etc. In addition, we have had a wealth of good, practical counsel from Ellen White in regard to children and money management education. The following examples are typical.

"Let every youth and every child be taught, not merely to solve imaginary problems, but to keep an accurate account of his own income and outgoes. Let him learn the right use of money by using it. Whether supplied by their parents or by their own earnings, let boys and girls learn to select and purchase their own clothing, their books, and other necessities; and by keeping an account of their expenses they will learn, as they could learn in no other way, the value and the use of money" (*Education*, pp. 238, 239).

The principles here are simple and basic. Parents should teach children to keep track of their income and expenses, whether their income is from their parents—an allowance—or money that they have earned themselves. Early on they should spend their money for basics—clothing, books, and personal items.

One thing we noted when the children began buying their own clothes was that they did not as often purchase the hottest brand-name items. The clones worked just as well. In addition, when our children shop they always first look through the sale items to see if any with special reduced prices would fit their needs. It almost goes without saying that when children purchase their own clothing they take better care of the garments by hanging them up after wearing and avoiding getting them damaged or soiled.

A question that parents frequently ask is "How old should children be when they begin to learn about money management?" Probably as soon as they are old enough to count. "When very young, children should be educated to read, to write, to understand figures, to keep their own accounts" (*Child Guidance,* p. 136).

I gather from this statement that right along with the three R's children must learn to manage their own money. Beyond that, they should know two other principles.

"Teach your children that God has a claim upon all they possess, and that nothing can ever cancel this claim; all they have is theirs only in trust, to prove whether they will be obedient. . . . Habits of economy, industry, and sobriety are, even in this world, a better portion for you and your children than a rich dowry" (*ibid.,* p. 134).

"[Children] are not to be carried along and supplied with money as if there were an inexhaustible supply from which they could draw to gratify every supposed need" (*The Adventist Home,* p. 386).

In addition to learning to keep track of income and expenses through the use of a simple budget and a checking account, children develop the habit of saving a portion of their income. They can learn the benefit of paying cash for purchases and of having interest work for you instead of against you. The burden of debt need never plague children if they learn good money management early.

Your children will not at first earn large amounts of money. It is, however, at that first income time that you must encourage them to be self-disciplined and begin their budgeting process by setting aside their tithe and offerings (as they did with their allowance).

When your children are teenagers, a family or church mission trip to a Third World country can be a powerful experience. Direct exposure to abject poverty can curb any complaints about food or living conditions at home and can initiate a lifetime of giving to the poor.

As children grow older and move farther down the road to independence, parents should provide new and more involved financial training. Assistance with the family budget and even role playing can help them learn how expensive it is to maintain a household.

It is not uncommon for young people to want to leave home a little prematurely. Generally they manifest it in the desire to "get an apartment and make it on my own." Frequently it is a very short-lived adventure when they learn that they are now responsible for the food, utilities, rent, clothing, etc. Quite commonly they return home after discovering that they had to do more than make the payments on the Camaro and the stereo. Obviously, it would be better to learn this lesson without having to experience it firsthand.

Vocational Planning

Vocational direction is critical in today's economy and expensive educational world. All too frequently young people go all the way through college and even graduate and never feel just right about their chosen major field of study. Many college graduates end up working in fields quite different than that for which they originally trained. To avoid such confusion and frustration, parents should assist their children in determining their skills, talents, or gifts, and the type of vocation that would best fit these qualities as well as their children's personality. In addition to vocational and aptitude testing, young people can also try to get summer jobs in the area of their interests or at least visit the types of work environment that their training would qualify them to pursue.

After God and lifework, a person's next major decision is a life companion. Since problems with money management, debt, and financial worries are the number one cause for marital difficulties and divorce, it goes without saying that premarital counseling and planning in the area of finance is vital. The chances for a happy and successful lifetime marriage will greatly increase when the partners are well-trained and self-disciplined in money management.

I would encourage every couple to prepare a one-year budget, then establish both short- and long-range financial goals. If couples can learn to work together for their goals, they can avoid the pitfalls into which so many fall.

Since every adult must face and deal with financial matters, learning to cope with them while under the guidance of experienced parents is one of the most important steps on the road to independence. We could compare passing our faith and experience on to the next generation to a relay race.

Any track coach will tell you that relay races are won or lost in the transferring of the baton from one runner to another. Seldom do sprinting athletes drop the baton once they have it firmly in their grasp. Losing it usually happens during the exchange between the runners. As parents, we have the responsibility to pass on the baton of the biblical principles of money management. At times it may seem as though we are not making much progress, but by being consistent, patient, and persistent, we can be successful.

APPLICATION
Chapter 7

1. What steps can parents take to aid their children on the road to financial independence?

2. What plan could a family follow to assure that their children finish college debt-free?

3. Why is it better to give children financial assistance when they are young than to give them a large amount when the parents die?

4. How do children learn and develop their habits of money management?

◆

CHAPTER EIGHT

"For which of you, intending to build a tower [house], does not sit down first and count the cost, whether he has enough to finish it—lest, after he has laid the foundation, and is not able to finish it, all who see it begin to mock him" (Luke 14:28, 29).

A Home of Your Own

A vital part of the American dream is owning your own home. It is not an easy process, and consequently many think that it's not worth the hassle. As a matter of fact, even though at the writing of this book the nation has the lowest interest rates in more than 20 years, the housing market is slow because of the still-inflated real estate prices and the debt load of the average family. Some economists predict that an even smaller number of families will be able to own their own homes in the near future.

In this chapter I will share with you the things I have learned over the past few years about the most intelligent ways to purchase a home. Tips that will aid you in a more informed use of your hard-owned money when planning to buy or build a home.

Single Largest Investment

Purchasing a home is no doubt the single largest investment most families ever make. Yet few have educated themselves on all the facts and financial obligations involved. Most only concern themselves with bank approval and whether or not they can make the payments.

Home buying is such an important transaction that you should do it only after a thorough investigation of the property, seeking the advice of an experienced real estate attorney, and a good working knowledge of how best to make a long-term purchase. You have to consider many factors. Location deserves high consideration—not only its proximity to work and school, but also the desirability of the neighborhood. Also you must take into account the quality of construction, the present condition of the home, environmental concerns, etc. In this chapter I am going to assume that you have considered all these factors and are now ready to purchase the home. Having made your best deal, you are satisfied with the price and just need to close the deal.

The vast majority of "homeowners" have a debt or mortgage on their homes. Here we will discuss methods of borrowing and how best to pay it back.

Because of the ready availability of credit and the general acceptance of debt as a way of life, home values have escalated radically over the past 20 years. Homes that cost around $25,000 in the sixties are $75,000 homes today. In some markets the escalation is even higher, and those same homes might cost $100,000-150,000.

How does a family harmonize Mrs. White's counsel to shun debt like the plague with her statements that we should seek the security of home ownership (see *The Adventist Home*, pp. 372, 373)? It's clear that she sees as the ideal situation a family finding a nice place in the country, away from the noise, crime, and pollution of the city, where the family members can enjoy times outdoors in the garden and yard and appreciate the beauties of nature. In my judgment the closer a family gets to this ideal, the happier and better adjusted they will be. But how should a family pay for such a dream house?

Let's face it, the average family today just doesn't have the $124,000 in cash that it would take to pay for the average home in America today. So generally it makes a trip (or many trips) to the bank to secure a loan for a major portion of the cost of the home. Later in the chapter I will share with you eight things to remember when borrowing money, especially a lot of money over a long period of time.

30-year Mortgages

Unless a person tells the banker differently, when applying for a home loan he or she will get a 30-year mortgage with—yes, count them—360 monthly payments. Now even 40-year mortgages are appearing. They do have lower monthly payments, but will, over the life of the loan, cost significantly more. For example, a $100,000, 30-year mortgage at 8.5 percent interest will have a monthly payment of $769, compared with only about $733 on a 40-year loan. But the 30-year mortgage will cost $276,840 in principal and interest over the term of the loan, compared with $351,840 for the 40-year note—a difference of $75,000!

Another problem with long mortgage amortization (payoff schedules) is that the average family doesn't just stick with one 30-year mortgage. After about 10 years of living in a home the couple will feel that they are now in a position where they can afford a larger or better home. They sell the first house and use their equity to make the down payment on the new home, but then go in debt for 30 years all over again. A couple years ago a report announced that in the large cities of Japan housing prices had shot up so high that the banks began offering 100-year mortgages. It would actually take three generations of people to pay off one loan!

As I mentioned in the early paragraphs of this book, both the Bible and Ellen White discourage long-term indebtedness. For example, in Deuteronomy 15:1 we read, "At the end of every seven years you shall grant a release of debts." Some have read the passage as permitting a form of bankruptcy in Old Testament times. Actually it is talking about something quite different. Instead of suggesting that the debtor did not have to pay his or her just obligations after seven years, what it does say is that the creditors should release the debtor then. The difference is important. The creditor, not the debtor, controlled the length of indebtedness. Let me explain it this way. Let's say that you are the banker and I am seeking a loan from you. What factors would you consider in setting up the loan? First you would examine my credit history, then determine the value of the item I was planning to purchase (appraisal); next you would research my job security and my ability to repay the loan, and finally you would check the calendar to see how many years remained on the seven-year cycle to determine the term of the loan. If we were three years into the seven-year cycle, then you would loan the money to me for only four years. The banker did not want to get caught holding the bag, as we say. The seven-year release discouraged long-term indebtedness.

The Biggers and the Smalls

For sake of illustration, let's use two hypothetical families to learn some of the principles of being a smart buyer. We'll call them the Biggers and the Smalls. Both families want a $100,000 house, both have incomes that will allow them to go forward with their plans, and both have $10,000 as a down payment. Now, for the next few paragraphs, consult Figure 4. Let's look first at the left-hand column and follow the Biggers' home purchase plan. The Biggers buy their $100,000 home by placing $10,000 down and financing $90,000 at 12 percent interest for 30 years. Their payments are $925.75 a month. At the end of 30 years the Biggers have paid $343,270 for their home.

The Smalls, on the other hand, while they don't fully understand the reason for the biblical limitation on long-term indebtedness, do want to manage their money using biblical principles. They purchase a smaller $60,000 house, put their $10,000 down, and finance the balance of $50,000 at 12 percent for seven years. Their payments are $882.64 per month. At the end of seven years they have completed the loan after investing $74,141 in it. Now they sell this house, apply $60,000 as a down payment on their $100,000 home, and finance the balance of $40,000 at 12 percent interest for seven years. This time their payments are $706.11 per month. At the end of seven years (14 years total) they have paid for their $100,000 home

HOW TO PURCHASE A HOUSE

Conventional 30 year vs. the Seven Year Plan

Biggers	Both want a $100,000 house	Smalls
$100,000	House	$60,000
- 10,000	Down Payment	- 10,000
$ 90,000	Balance	$50,000
12% / 30 years	Terms	12% / 7 years
$925.75 / month	Payment	$882.64 / month

7 years paid in full: $74,141

$100,000
-   60,000
$ 40,000

12% / 7 years

$706.11 / month
7 years paid in full: $59,313

After 30 years

Biggers		Smalls
$333,270	Amount Paid	$133,454*
---0---	Amount saved first 7 yrs.	$5,214.74
---0---	Amount saved after 14 yrs.	$36,950.04
---0---	Total saved after 30 years.	$615,809.99**

**Note these calculations were generated on a computer using a 10% rate of return compounded monthly. During the first 7-year cycle the Smalls invested the difference between their monthly payment and that of the Biggers ($43.11) and the same during the second 7-year cycle with the difference of $219.64 per month. Then after 14 years when their house was fully paid off, they invested the entire amount of the Biggers' monthly payment — $925.75. The total investment of the Smalls from their savings in home mortgage expenses over the Biggers would be $615,809.99 cash in the bank!

*In addition, note that even if the Smalls did not follow the investment program outlined above, they still have $199,815.82 less invested in their home than the Biggers ($333,270.00 less $133,454.00). That's nearly $200,000.00 that they could invest in their needs, the needs of others, and to advancing the cause of God.

Figure 4

through the use of the equity in the first home and an additional $59,313. So at the end of 14 years the Smalls have their $100,000 house paid for at a cost of $143,454 ($10,000 plus $74,141 plus $59,313). It is a savings of nearly $200,000 over what the Biggers will put into their house.

But the savings don't end there. The Smalls invested the difference between their monthly payments and those of the Biggers during the 14 years they were each paying on their home and then invested the amount of the total monthly payment of the Biggers during the last 16 years of the Biggers' mortgage (figured at 10 percent interest). Then at the end of the 30 years the Biggers and the Smalls get together to celebrate the Biggers finally getting their house paid off. Probably the Smalls are taking the Biggers out to supper. When they compare notes (pun intended), they find that the Biggers have their house paid off with 360 payment stubs to prove it, for which they spent $343,270. The Smalls also have their house paid off, for which they paid $143,454, but in addition, they also have $615,809 dollars in the bank! It is unlikely that a self-sacrificing Christian would keep that much money in the bank, but you get the point. Evidently there really is some benefit to short-term indebtedness. And think of the surplus funds that would be available to help others and to advance the cause of God.

Principles of Borrowing

There are a number of other ways perhaps more useful in today's economy that one can utilize to save money on a home purchase. Before we look at them in detail, however, let me share some general principles that one should consider when contemplating any type of borrowing.

1. Borrow as little as possible.

Many times when people go to the bank for money they rationalize that "while I am getting the loan, I might as well get enough to pay for this and this and this." Don't! Always borrow as little as possible.

2. Make the payback term as short as possible.

The monthly payment for many families is the major criterion for the loan. However, I believe that it is wise to have the bank spell out several amortization options for you so that you can choose the one best for you. For example, for a $60,000 loan one can pay it off in 15 years instead of 30 just by adding a little more than $100 each month. It is always good to inquire what the payment would be if you financed for 15 years instead of the standard 30 years. Merchants take advantage of the monthly payment mentality. Glance at the new car advertisements in the Sunday paper. Many state that the monthly payment is say $299 per month without bothering to mention the total cost of the car or the time it takes to pay it off—usually five years.

3. Have a fixed rate of interest.

While interest rates do fall during recessionary periods, historically they tend to go up rather than down. Here is the problem. Interest rates will normally increase sometime over the life of the mortgage, so your interest and monthly payment will also rise. An adjustable-rate mortgage puts the borrower at risk. Fixed-rate loans, on the other hand, place the risk on the lender.

4. Be sure there is no prepayment penalty.

Your goal for any loan should be to pay it off as quickly as possible to escape the burden of debt and to save interest costs. If you have a prepayment penalty, then if you attempt to prepay part or all of your loan, you may still have to pay all or part of the interest anyway. Several families have contacted me over the past couple years with a serious problem with their auto loans. Here is the situation. Some states have now passed laws that allow creditors (the lenders) who make auto loans to charge the customer (debtor) all of the interest on the loan no matter when you pay it off. The law requires that they disclose that fact to you at the time you sign for the loan, but many customers fail to read or understand it. Let me illustrate: Let's say you buy a new car with a small down payment and finance $15,000 at 10 percent simple interest for five years (60 payments). After making the payments for one year, you come into some extra money and decide to pay the car off. The standard procedure is to call the lending institution and ask for a payoff, to which the clerk would say something like "Well, if you pay it off by next Monday your payoff (the balance of the principal of your loan) would be $12,565.92." However, under the new laws in some states the clerk would simply tell you to tear out all the remaining coupons (the 48 payments left), add them up, and send in a check for the total. This would mean that instead of saving the $2,731.80 interest that you would have paid if you continued to make the regular monthly payments, you now add this amount to your principal balance and your payoff is $15,297.72, more than you financed in the first place!

This is such an important point that I want you to see it from another perspective. Imagine you visit a model home in a new subdivision one Sunday afternoon. The salesperson tells you that if you buy one of their homes by the fifteenth of the current month, you will get a free refrigerator with the home. Do you really get a free refrigerator? Maybe, and maybe not! Some will conclude that the construction company will charge you for it some way. But that is not the point here. They could be giving you a bona fide incentive. Here is the point. If you decide to make the purchase, note the bold printing just above the signature line on the contract. It will say words to this effect: **No oral or verbal representations by any sales agent**

or representative of the seller are binding unless a part of this written contract. So check that the contract actually mentions the free refrigerator. Otherwise you probably won't get one.

Now, let's apply this to the purchase of a home. You are sitting around the conference table at the bank or title company at the "closing" of your loan agreement. Usually an attorney will be present. Who is that attorney representing? Not you. He or she looks after the interests of the seller or the lending institution. So the closing agent goes through all the documents with you and then asks if you understand everything. Most people, to avoid appearing ignorant or from fear that any questions may jeopardize the loan, reply yes. But you should always ask whether or not the contract has a prepayment penalty. If the closing agent says no, then inquire where it states that in the documents. If the documents are not clear, have them insert it boldly into the contract before signing it. Only then will you be able to save interest by prepaying principal.

5. Avoid personal surety.

As we discussed earlier in chapter 5, the Bible tells us to avoid personal surety. While this is not always possible, you should try to have the object for which you are borrowing be the full security and not any of your other assets. When purchasing a car or a home, you will need a considerable down payment (perhaps 40 percent or more) before the lender will release a borrower from personal surety.

6. Shop for the money.

Money is a commodity that you can purchase for varying rates of interest. Don't just settle for the bank that you always do business with. Closing costs and interest rates vary from lender to lender. Make sure that you are making the best deal for you.

7. Do not purchase credit life insurance.

The problems with credit life insurance are many. First of all, it has the highest commission for the salesperson of any form of insurance. Up to 60 percent of the premium goes to the salesperson. In addition, one must die to collect benefits. And that brings up another problem. The only benefit to the insured is the payoff of the specific loan covered. Let me illustrate. Imagine you purchase credit life insurance on the $15,000 loan you took out to buy the car we talked about above under number 4. If you die after having made 59 payments, how much benefit will your estate realize? Not $15,000. Only the final payment will go to the loan company. From my perspective, the best coverage for existing debt is one simple term life insurance policy to cover all your debts. It is much cheaper to purchase, plus it will pay your estate the entire face amount of the policy.

8. Know what you are doing.

When you seek a loan, be assertive. Don't act like the bank is doing you a favor. If no one borrowed money, they would go out of business. So approach the bank with a knowledge of the above pointers plus current market conditions. When talking with the loan officer, you could say something like "I/we are planning to purchase a home and are out shopping for the money. We are looking for a competitive interest rate and a minimum of closing costs. Also we want to pay the loan off as quickly as possible to save interest costs, so we insist that there be no prepayment penalty. Are you interested in working with us?"

An illustration here may be helpful. Suppose that on the morning of the day you enter the bank seeking a loan, the interest drops one full percentage point, from 10 to 9 percent. The banker does not have to disclose this to you and probably won't if you appear to be eager for approval. If, on the other hand, you are assertive, he or she will share the new lower rate plan with you in order to get your business. And you'll end up saving thousands over the course of your loan payback.

I hope these points will be helpful to you. Being debt-free is by far the best plan, but if you must borrow for your home or business, do so in an intelligent manner.

Paying a Mortgage More Quickly

Now, as I conclude this chapter I want to give you some practical advice on better and quicker ways to pay back a home mortgage. Everywhere I share this with people they are amazed and upset that they didn't know about this 20 years earlier. You see, the average person who gets a 30-year home mortgage feels that the only option is faithfully making all 360 payments one month at a time. But I happen to believe there are many better ways to pay them off.

When the customer makes all 360 monthly payments, the picture looks like this: A couple gets married and buys a home with a 30-year mortgage. Then they start their family, send their kids to school, clear through college. The kids leave home and begin families of their own, and Mom and Dad are still paying on their home. And for the vast majority the problem is even worse, because most families sell their first or second homes and use the equity to put down on another home and finance it for an additional 30 years. Accordingly, many find themselves making house payments even after retirement.

Now, let's consider some practical suggestions for mortgage payoff. First study Figure 5, where we will look at a $60,000 mortgage at 12 percent interest from various perspectives. The chart contains five columns. The first is the type of loan, and the second, the payment amount. P/I simply means

COMPARE A $60,000
MORTGAGE
AT 12%

	P/I	LIFE OF LOAN	INTEREST PAID	INTEREST SAVED
CONVENTIONAL	$ 617.17	30	$162,181.20	-0-
BI-WEEKLY	$ 308.59	19.04	$ 92,752.05	$ 69,429.15
WEEKLY	$ 154.29	18.79	$ 90,809.33	$ 71,372.20
15 YEAR	$ 720.10	15	$ 69,618.45	$ 92,562.75
BI-WEEKLY	$ 360.05	12.3	$ 54,617.36	$107,563.84
7 YEAR	$1,059.16	7	$ 28,969.95	$133,211.25

Figure 5

principal (the amount of the payment that goes to reduce your loan balance) and interest (the money you give the bank for the privilege of using their funds). The third column is the length of the loan in number of years. The fourth is the amount of interest you will pay over the life of the loan. And the fifth column is the amount of interest you would save over the conventional loan on the top line as compared to any of the other options.

The first line shows a conventional 30-year mortgage. The monthly payment is $617.17, and the amount of interest paid to the bank on the payback is $162,181.20. The $60,000 loan amount will be paid back in full in all the types considered here, so I have left that amount out of the table.

Now go to line 2—the biweekly repayment plan. By just doing one simple thing, you can save thousands of dollars in interest during the life of the loan and cut way back on the time it takes to complete the loan. Here is how the biweekly plan works. First, divide the regular monthly payment in half. In this case it would be $617.17 divided by 2. The new payment amount is $308.59. Now you can forget about monthly payments altogether and simply pay half a monthly payment every two weeks. By doing this one simple thing you cut the time of the payback to 19 years, thereby saving yourself 11 years' worth of payments and nearly $70,000 in interest.

How does it work? It's simple, really. By making a payment every two weeks, you actually make 26 of the "half payments" per year, equivalent to making 13 regular monthly payments. The big advantage comes when you realize that the thirteenth payment goes 100 percent to the principal to reduce the balance on your loan. By the way, if you are already involved in a mortgage repayment plan and your bank refuses to change your loan to a biweekly plan of repayment, you can get a similar benefit (assuming, of course, that you will not incur any prepayment penalty) in this way: Divide your current monthly payment by 12 and add that amount to each month's regular payment. Be sure to note on your check that the extra amount is to be applied to the principal. For a $60,000 30-year loan at 12 percent this means adding an extra $51.43 to the normal $617.17, making a total monthly check of $668.60. By doing this you would save $69,178.92 in interest and 10 years and 11 months' worth of payments.

I have heard some people say, "My CPA told me not to pay my house off early because I need the interest deduction on my income tax return." If your CPA tells you that, you know (unless you are a minister) that it is time to get a new CPA. The bottom line is that when all is said and done you will have more money by paying the taxes on your income than by paying out all that interest over the years. In addition, you are receiving a tax deduction for all the mortgage interest you do pay during the course of the year. You can check out the other options on your own, but let's examine just one more alternative on the chart. Look at the fourth line—the 15-year loan. Note that under this plan, by simply adding an additional $103 per month to the monthly payment, you can pay your loan off in half the time and save yourself more than $92,000 in interest.

Finally, I want to share with you the dramatic results you can achieve by having a copy of your loan payoff schedule balance, what accountants call an amortization schedule (see Figure 6). Here we have the same loan we considered in Figure 5—a $60,000 loan at 12 percent interest for a 30-year payback. The monthly payment is $617.17. The bank uses the amortization schedule to keep track of your payments and declining balance. Generated by a computer, it allows you to see the entire payback schedule of your loan at one time. On this particular schedule, if you made all the payments according to schedule, the last one would occur in December of the year 2022. I have reproduced only the first two years for this illustration, but you understand that it actually has 30 yearly segments in the complete amortization schedule instead of the two shown in Figure 6.

Amortization Schedules

Now we shall turn our attention to the amortization schedule so that we can become familiar with it and thus utilize it to our best advantage. First, you will note that the schedule contains five columns. The first has the

Principal: $60,000.00   % Rate: 12.000   Years: 30
MONTHLY Payment: $617.17
FINAL est. Payment: $608.64

Date	No.	Interest	Principal	Balance
1/1993	1	600.00	17.17	59,982.83
2/1993	2	599.83	17.34	59,965.49
3/1993	3	599.65	17.52	59,947.97
4/1993	4	599.48	17.69	59,930.28
5/1993	5	599.30	17.87	59,912.41
6/1993	6	599.12	18.05	59,894.36
7/1993	7	598.94	18.23	59,876.13
8/1993	8	598.76	18.41	59,857.72
9/1993	9	598.58	18.59	59,839.13
10/1993	10	598.39	18.78	59,820.35
11/1993	11	598.20	18.97	59,801.38
12/1993	12	598.01	19.16	59,782.22
	1993 Totals	**7,188.26**	**217.78**	
1/1994	13	597.82	19.35	59,762.87
2/1994	14	597.63	19.54	59,743.33
3/1994	15	597.43	19.74	59,723.59
4/1994	16	597.24	19.93	59,703.66
5/1994	17	597.04	20.13	59,683.53
6/1994	18	596.84	20.33	59,663.20
7/1994	19	596.63	20.54	59,642.66
8/1994	20	596.43	20.74	59,621.92
9/1994	21	596.22	20.95	59,600.97
10/1994	22	596.01	21.16	59,579.81
11/1994	23	595.80	21.37	59,558.44
12/1994	24	595.58	21.59	59,536.85
	1994 Totals	**7,160.67**	**245.37**	
1/1995	25	595.37	21.80	59,515.05
2/1995	26	595.15	22.02	59,493.03
3/1995	27	594.93	22.24	59,470.79
4/1995	28	594.71	22.46	59,448.33
5/1995	29	594.48	22.69	59,425.64
6/1995	30	594.26	22.91	59,402.73
7/1995	31	594.03	23.14	59,379.59
8/1995	32	593.80	23.37	59,356.22
9/1995	33	593.56	23.61	59,332.61
10/1995	34	593.33	23.84	59,308.77
11/1995	35	593.09	24.08	59,284.69
12/1995	36	592.85	24.32	59,260.37
	1995 Totals	**7,129.56**	**276.48**	

month and year due date of the payment. The second contains the number of the payment, starting with 1 and ending with 360. The third column indicates the amount of interest in each payment—the amount you give the bank for the privilege of borrowing the money. The fourth column disclosure the principal, the amount of your monthly payment that actually reduces the balance of your loan. Please note that columns 3 and 4— interest and principal—always add up to $617.17, the amount of the total monthly payment. The fifth and final column is the balance column, telling you how much money you still owe after making that particular payment. So for a quick review, look at the top line of the amortization schedule. Note that payment 1 comes due in January of 1993, and when you make that payment, $600.00 goes to the bank and only $17.17 applies to your loan, leaving an unpaid balance of $59,982.83.

That first line appears kind of discouraging, doesn't it? But let me share with you some ways that you can take advantage of this information. In the past, while counseling a family, I have suggested that they double up on mortgage payments. The couples generally reply, "We can barely make our $617.17 monthly payment, so there is no way we could double it and pay $1,234.34 each month." But by looking at the payment schedule you can easily see that it is much easier than you think to make extra payments. First, remember that the interest is calculated on the unpaid balance, so each month the interest due for that period of time appears in column 3. Then you can pay as much on the principal to reduce your loan as you want to as long as you face no prepayment penalty. For example, if in January of 1993 when you made your first payment of $617.17, note that $600.00 of interest was due and $17.17 went to your loan. If at the time you made the January payment you had added just the principal due for the next month, which was $17.34, you would have paid payment 2 in full and saved yourself $599.83. That is interest you would have had to pay if you had waited until the next month to pay payment 2. So now your next payment is actually payment 3.

Now look at the 1993 total line. You can see that after making 12 monthly payments of $617.17, you would have given the bank $7,188.26 and reduced your loan by only $217.78, leaving a balance at the end of the first year of $59,782.22. Next quickly glance down at the totals for 1994. Note that at the end of the 12 payments in 1994 you will have in that year alone given the bank $7,160.67 and reduced the loan by only $245.37. Stay with me now. If in December of 1993 when you made your regular payment you had added the total principal amount that you would pay during the 12 payments of 1994—the $245.37 figure—you would just have paid all 12 payments of 1994, and your next payment would be number 25.

By investing the extra $245.37 in your home mortgage, you would have saved yourself $7,160.67 in interest that you would have otherwise had to pay.

Not only do you cut a year off the length of your mortgage payback, but you also get a tremendous return on your investment. If you divide the amount of interest that you saved ($7,160.67) by the amount of the extra principal you paid ($245.37), it goes in 29 times. That is a 29 to 1 return on your investment! Even more dramatic is the fact that this represents a return on investment of 2,800 percent. Amazing, isn't it?

Many question these tremendous figures when they first hear them. But to prove it to yourself, all you have to do is compare the total columns of 1993 and 1994. Note that at the end of 1993 the unpaid balance is $59,782.22. However, if you reduce that amount by the total amount of principal that you would normally pay in 1994 ($245.37), then your 1993 ending balance is $59,536.85, so you save the $7,160.67 in interest that you would have otherwise paid in 1994, and your next payment after number 12 is number 25!

IRAs

This leads us to another startling revelation. We have all heard of IRAs—individual retirement accounts. Under the IRA plan an employee can deposit up to $2,000 per year tax-free in an approved account as an investment for retirement. A number of restrictions apply, but I won't go into that here. But just for the sake of interest, let's say that you could invest your $2,000 at 10 percent as I did with the Smalls in the illustration above. In today's economy that would be a good rate of return. But now suppose that you would consider placing that $2,000 as a payment on the principal of your home mortgage. You can make extra principal payments at any time, but for sake of illustration it is easier for me to explain the process if we do it at a year-end break point.

So let's go back to December of 1993 on the amortization schedule (Figure 6). If with your December payment of $617.17 you added $2,025.89 to be applied to the principal of your loan (just $25.89 more than the standard IRA contribution), you would have just accomplished by this single act a savings of six years off the length of your mortgage and escaped $42,410.38 dollars in interest payments. It offers a return on your investment of nearly 21 to 1, or 2,000 percent! Why would anyone ever put money into an IRA while still owing money on a home?

Some have said, "I have been told that this works only in the first year or two of the mortgage, so it is too late for us to get any benefit from accelerated principal payments." Don't believe it! It is nearly always to your benefit to prepay debts. Most people mistakenly assume that after the first 15 years of a loan payoff, most of their monthly payment reduces the balance of their loan and only a smaller portion goes to the bank as interest. Not so! In the amortization schedule shown in Figure 6 not until April of the year 2017—24.5 years into the 30-year mortgage—would you begin having more of your payment apply to principal than interest! So even 24.5 years into the mortgage you could still make two payments by paying a full payment and half of another one.

Paying off your home offers many benefits. As I will point out in the chapter about retirement, if you have your home paid off, you can reduce by the amount of a monthly payment what you will need to sustain you in retirement. In addition, many counselors now recognize that one of the best ways to plan ahead for the cost of your children's college education is to pay off your home mortgage. Once you get it paid off, you can then begin using the money previously required for mortgage payments to assist with education expenses.

In summary, let me state that once you have eliminated your consumer debts and put aside reasonable savings (three to six months' income equivalent), then you can maximize your efforts to pay off your home. Have a plan and work it. I believe that your money is just as safe in your home as it is in the banks. Even if the economy fails and the real estate market turns down, at least you will have a place to live.

Finally, remember: "We are not to feel disturbed if our neighbors build and furnish their houses in a manner that we are not authorized to follow" (*The Adventist Home*, p. 384). We do not need elaborate homes here. God is preparing our mansions in heaven. By being prudent in our investments and minimizing our debt, we can free up more funds to answer the urgent calls for funds to take advantage of the mission openings available to us today. May God bless you as you prayerfully consider your housing situation.

APPLICATION
Chapter 8

1. How long is the typical home mortgage payback in years? What length does the Bible suggest as the longest anyone should be in debt? (See Deuteronomy 15:1.)

2. What advantages can you list for prepaying your home mortgage?

3. Why should you insist that there be no prepayment penalty on your home mortgage or any other money you borrow?

◆

CHAPTER NINE

"I have been young, and now am old; yet I have not seen the righteous forsaken, nor his descendants begging bread" (Psalm 37:25).

Working for the Gold Watch

Retirement! The word conjures up all kinds of images to the working person. And quite often nightmares of a different kind to many who have "retired." The phenomenon is a relatively modern invention. Retirement advisors are making a killing peddling advice on how and when to retire and—most important—where to invest your money.

Many see retirement as the culmination of the American dream. Others with a contrary opinion state, "A retirement to a life of ease and pleasure has been the world's alternative to heaven. It has not worked. Multitudes of retired people have discovered the shocking truth that to lose your usefulness is to invite rejection.

"There may be a place in later years for a change in vocation, but never did God intend for there to be a ceasing of labor. This was made quite clear in man's beginning, when God said to Adam that he must work until the day he died. 'In the sweat of thy face shalt thou eat bread, till thou return unto the ground' (Genesis 3:19)" (*Men's Manual,* Institute in Basic Youth Conflicts, vol. 2, p. 252).

In this chapter we will look at the later years in life and how we can complete them with the least frustration and a sense of true satisfaction. We will examine what the Bible and Ellen White say about retirement, how the uncertain financial conditions of our present state of society affect retirement security, the state of the Social Security system, and some suggestions on how best to cope with these situations.

Let me warn you that looking ahead to retirement, about 15 years for people my age, uncovers a bleak picture. I will explain the problems in some detail later in this chapter. But let me assure you that God has a plan for this time of our lives, and He will see us through. Jesus, in Matthew 6:25-34, exhorts us to make sure that we put our dependence upon God and not on the things of this world:

"Therefore I say to you, do not worry about your life, what you will eat or what you will drink; nor about your body, what you will put on. Is not life more than food and the body more than clothing? Look at the birds of the air, for they neither sow nor reap nor gather into barns; yet your heavenly Father feeds them. Are you not of more value than they? Which of you by worrying can add one cubit to his stature? So why do you worry about clothing? Consider the lilies of the field, how they grow; they neither toil nor spin; and yet I say to you that even Solomon in all his glory was not arrayed like one of these. Now if God so clothes the grass of the field, which today is, and tomorrow is thrown into the oven, will He not much more clothe you, O you of little faith? Therefore do not worry, saying, 'What shall we eat?' or 'What shall we drink?' or 'What shall we wear?' For after all these things the Gentiles seek. For your heavenly Father knows that you need all these things. But seek first the kingdom of God and His righteousness, and all these things shall be added to you. Therefore do not worry about tomorrow, for tomorrow will worry about its own things. Sufficient for the day is its own trouble."

Worries About the Future

As people get older, they almost naturally begin to worry about the future. If you find yourself tempted in this regard, read again the passage quoted above from Jesus' sermon on the mount. The things that usually concern us about the future are:

1. Dying too soon—before the family is taken care of.
2. Living too long—outlasting assets or savings.
3. Catastrophic illness—all resources could go at one time.
4. Mental and/or physical disability—who will take care of me.

Insurance companies make fortunes on these common fears of older people. We voluntarily give insurance companies billions of dollars annually to provide a sense of security. Of course, in addition to the money spent on insurance, which may be reasonable in moderation, people hoard money as well, since "you never know what may happen in the future." We will talk about hoarding and investments in some detail in chapter 11.

Some time ago during my devotional reading I found an interesting passage in which Ellen White comments on these fears.

"Satan often plays upon their [aged persons'] imagination and leads them to feel a continual anxiety in regard to their money. It is their idol, and they hoard it with miserly care. They will sometimes deprive themselves of many of the comforts of life, and labor beyond their strength, rather than use the means which they have. In this way they place themselves in continual want, through fear that sometime in the future they shall want. *All these fears originate with Satan.* . . . If they would take the position which

God would have them, their last days might be their best and happiest. . . . They should lay aside anxiety and burdens, and occupy their time as happily as they can, and be ripening up for heaven" *(Testimonies,* vol. 1, pp. 423, 424; italics supplied).

What is God's plan for our personal and financial security? In addition to Matthew 6:33 (quoted above), the Bible has several other choice promises:

"Be anxious for nothing, but in everything by prayer and supplication, with thanksgiving, let your requests be made known to God. . . . And my God shall supply all your need according to His riches in glory by Christ Jesus" (Philippians 4:6-19).

"Offer to God thanksgiving, and pay your vows to the Most High. Call upon Me in the day of trouble; I will deliver you, and you shall glorify Me" (Psalm 50:14, 15).

"Command those who are rich in this present age not to be haughty, nor to trust in uncertain riches but in the living God, who gives us richly all things to enjoy" (1 Timothy 6:17).

Commenting on Matthew 6:33, Ellen White amplifies the promise contained there by saying, "Open your hearts to receive [God's] kingdom, and make its service your highest interest. Though it is a spiritual kingdom, fear not that your needs for this life will be uncared for. If you give yourself to God's service, He who has all power in heaven and earth will provide for your needs" *(Thoughts From the Mount of Blessing,* p. 99).

What great promises we have, and what an even greater God who made them. But alas, what great faith it takes for us to claim them!

The Bible and Retirement

The Bible does not say much about retirement. In fact, sometimes I will ask a seminar group with a twinkle in my eye, so they think it is a trick question, "You folks know what the Bible says about retirement, don't you?" Generally they respond with just silence, and after a few seconds I will say, "Everyone is absolutely correct. It says nothing."

In two places in the Bible older people make a change in their lifestyle, but the most common plan was to work as long as one could and then become a counselor to younger people.

Let's quickly look at the two situations in the Bible. The only Old Testament reference to my knowledge is Numbers 8:25: "And at the age of fifty years they [the Levites] must cease performing this work, and shall work no more." It is not much of a foundation on which to build a case for the retirement system we have today, particularly since the Temple priests referred to in this passage then took on other priestly duties.

Then there is the New Testament example of "retirement" in Luke 12.

As Jesus taught one day, a man in the crowd interrupted His sermon and asked Him to tell his brother to divide their inheritance with him. Jesus responded, "Take heed and beware of covetousness, for one's life does not consist in the abundance of the things he possesses" (verse 15), and then to the crowd that had gathered He recounted the parable of the man who retired—the rich fool. When blessed beyond his needs and capacity to store, instead of sharing with others less fortunate, the man chose to build bigger barns, store up his "wealth," and stop working. After the rich fool built the bigger barns, Jesus tells us three things:

First, the man decided to keep all the blessing to himself, stop working, and live it up. "And I will say to my soul, 'Soul, you have many goods laid up for many years; take your ease; eat, drink, and be merry'" (verse 19). In modern language, he said, "I have enough saved up to last me for a long time. I think I'll take early retirement, buy a motor home, and tour the country."

Second, Jesus pronounced a judgment. "But God said to him, 'You fool! This night your soul will be required of you; then whose will those things be which you have provided?'" (verse 20). I believe here Jesus pointed out that since we do not know the day of our death, we should always be ready for it by living to carry out God's will instead of a life of selfishness.

Third, Jesus makes the application to His audience. "So is he who lays up treasure for himself, and is not rich toward God" (verse 21). Jesus here echoes Matthew 6:19, 20, where He says, "Do not lay up for yourselves treasures on earth . . . ; but lay up for yourselves treasures in heaven." I'll talk about these verses in more detail in chapter 11.

The general picture in the Bible is that one works and remains productive as long as he or she is able; then his family assists him or her until death. In fact, for those who appreciate the two great prophetic books, Daniel and the Revelation, it is interesting to note that both had authors in their 80s at a time when the average person didn't live beyond their 20s or 30s.

Larry Burkett illustrates this idea with the example of the apostle Paul. "He had certainly served his time in the service of the Lord even before he began his third missionary journey. No one would have faulted him if he had elected to retire at Corinth or Ephesus and write his memoirs. He might even have returned to his Mediterranean home near the city of Tarsus and lived out his remaining years in peace. Yet he chose to continue his journeys, giving no thought about retirement as long as he was able to perform the duties God assigned him. At this time Paul was probably in his late 60s, ancient by the standards of his generation" (Larry Burkett,

Answers to Your Questions About Retirement, pp. 6, 7).

Older Employees — Valuable Asset

Ellen White taught and practiced the principle of using the experience of older employees as a valuable asset to the work of God. In 1990 the White Estate released a compilation entitled *The Retirement Years.* Urging younger men to value the experience of older leaders, she stated, "And let no aged worker, although he is old and gray, think that he is released from service" (p. 31). "My brethren in the ministry, it is better, far better, to die of hard work in some home or foreign mission field, than to rust out with inaction" (p. 39). She practiced what she preached. Ellen White wrote many of her best-known and -loved books like *The Desire of Ages* after age 70.

Social Security

In the past people felt quite secure in their post-work years, resting on the three-legged stool of Social Security, a pension, and some personal savings. However, the picture is changing. "When Social Security was enacted in 1935 and retirement was set at 65, the average male that age could expect to live an additional 12 years. Today he could expect to live about 15 years, and by 2025, the figure could be 20 years. And since these life expectancies are average, a good many of those folks will need to support themselves even longer. At the same time, the age at which full Social Security benefits can be collected will rise to 67, and the portion of benefits you sacrifice when you retire early will be greater" (*U.S. News & World Report*, Aug. 14, 1989, p. 55). It is clear to many financial counselors that the retiree of the future may need to add a fourth leg to his retirement stool—a job!

With the state of our federal economy at present, most counselors are beginning to warn, "Don't rely on the government for your retirement." They base it on the following types of reasons:

1. The tremendous debt load on the government. When George Bush took office, he stated that during his first term he would balance the federal budget. However, his first budget was $65 billion in the red, and it went from bad to worse. Of course, he didn't count on the collapse of the savings and loan industry, which added another $500 billion-plus to the problem. In addition, the nation has had to face the expense of the Persian Gulf war, Hurricane Andrew, lower revenues from taxes because of the high unemployment brought on by the recession, etc. With more than 4 trillion in debt, the government is actuarily bankrupt, but it can't just declare bankruptcy, pass go, and collect $200, because we owe most of the debt to foreign countries like Japan. As I mentioned in an earlier chapter, many economists predict that because we are now borrowing to pay the interest on the national debt, the compounding effect of the debt will, in less than seven years, require all the revenues generated by the tax system just to service the interest on the national debt. You can only imagine the effect this will have on society when the welfare, Social Security, and the entitlement programs go unfunded.

2. The welfare burden. In 1935, when (following the Great Depression) the government established the welfare system, for each person drawing welfare benefits 143 people worked. Now the ratio is one to one! There is one person drawing some form of welfare or entitlement money for each person employed. In addition, the delivery system and the criminal element are exploiting the system as well. Today more than 13 million people subsist entirely from the welfare system, the highest number in the history of the program.

3. The Social Security system is insecure. "If you were born after 1936, don't count on Social Security to make your retirement years comfortable. The Social Security system will be in serious trouble within 10 years, and the crunch will be devastating when the baby boomers start arriving at retirement age around 2010.

"Social Security has expanded coverage and benefits so much that this year it will pay out $302 billion! That is $830 million a day to retired workers and their spouses, widows and dependent children, and the disabled.

"As matters now stand, there simply will not be enough money to pay promised benefits" (*Bottom Line Personal*, vol. 13, No. 19 [Oct. 15, 1992].

You may have heard some say that the Social Security system has enough money to last for 20 more years and others claim the system is broke. What is the truth? They are both right. On paper the system has a good surplus. However, law requires that the extra funds be invested in special issue government bonds that are then sold to pay interest on the national debt. The money is all gone! We only have IOUs from the government. Those presently working are paying in to assist those drawing benefits.

4. The graying of America. In just a few years when the baby boomers begin to retire, the nation will have twice as many people retired as today, and only half as many working. It will have a devastating effect on the economy.

5. One third of a nation. In May of 1988 the Commission on Minority Participation in Education and American Life presented its report to the president of the United States in a book entitled *One Third of a Nation*. The bottom line is that unless the United States does something drastic to the American educational system, by the year 2000 one third of the work force

will be minorities—Blacks, Hispanics, Asians, and American Indians—
who for whatever reason have not been able to avail themselves of the
educational system and will be laboring at minimum wage. Imagine, one
third of our work force employed at below subsistence income. I have
helped many families work out a budget and turn things around financially.
But unless a family is completely debt-free (including no home mortgage),
it is nearly impossible to develop a family budget on minimum wage.
Minimum wage is primarily for entry-level jobs for young people and older
men and women who need to supplement their income.

6. The abortion and declining birthrate problem. Since the 1973
U.S. Supreme Court decision in *Roe v. Wade* that essentially legalized
abortion on demand, conservative estimates suggest that nearly 25 million
fetuses have been aborted. The present pro-life or pro-choice controversy is
being fought over ethics, morality, and constitutional rights. Yet the present
battle seems to overlook entirely another aspect of the abortion question.
Given the above statistic, we have sacrificed an entire generation of people
that could have been around to support us when we are old. The
homosexual community produces no children for the next generation. In
addition, many professional couples are opting for either no children or a
single child. All this underscores the fact that the work force will shrink
drastically as the present generation of workers retires.

I realize that this is a very depressing view of the future. However, I
believe it is an accurate one. The primary question, then, is what can one do
to prepare for the future when he or she will not be able to be gainfully
employed.

Obviously, all of us at some point in time begin to lose our physical and
mental capabilities. How do we prepare for that time? Financial gurus tell
us that in order to retire with a comfortable retirement income, one must
have at least $400,000 in investments. What is the best way to prepare for
retirement—especially in the light of our present economy and our setting
in eschatological time? Let me share a few suggestions.

I believe that the very first prerequisite to retirement is to plan on being
debt-free. When you have your primary source of income cut off, it is no
time to be in debt. As I mentioned in chapter 8, assuming you have
adequate savings for your current budget needs, I would always
recommend paying off your home mortgage early if possible. Once you
have eliminated your mortgage, you can invest those funds if you need
additional assistance for retirement. That way you own your own home no
matter what, and you will have reduced your retirement income needs by
the amount of your former monthly payments.

As we previously mentioned, one of the major concerns as people grow older is their health and their health insurance. Many have thought to themselves, *If I had known that I was going to live this long, I would have taken better care of myself.* So start today to evaluate your present health habits and if necessary modify your lifestyle to ensure a proper health maintenance program. I would highly recommend a visit to one of the fine lifestyle programs at an institution such as Weimar, Wildwood, or Yuchi Pines. Here you could get an education that would serve you well in the future. Contact the ASI office at the General Conference for the address of the institution nearest to you.

From the standpoint of overall health, it is to your advantage to enter retirement at your ideal weight. Being overweight is a risk factor in hypertension, heart disease, diabetes, and even some forms of cancer. In addition, being overweight reduces the likelihood that you will participate in a regular exercise program. In short, maintain ideal weight, eat a well-balanced vegetarian diet, and have a regular exercise program. Obviously, by living a healthy lifestyle you will add to both the quality and length of your life.

Where to Retire

Where you choose to live during your retirement is also vital. The following are areas of concern when you begin living on a lower income:

1. The climate. A place like Land Between the Lakes, in Kentucky, has average temperatures and humidity of 47.8 degrees and 69 percent. You get four great seasons, including a good growing season, and it's never too hot or too cold. This means good savings on utility costs.

2. Affordable cost of living. Look for a place where you can live comfortably for under $25,000 per year. I am most familiar with the rural South. Try Kentucky, Tennessee, Georgia, or North Carolina. Other parts of the country will have their low cost of living areas.

3. Low-priced housing. If you currently live because of preference or work necessity in an area that has high-priced housing—such as the Washington, D.C., area, California, or the East Coast, consider moving. Take advantage of your one-time capital gains tax break when you are past age 55, and use the equity in your home to pay cash for a home in one of the areas listed above. You may even have some cash left over to purchase your retirement car and put some in savings!

4. Health care. One factor in choosing your retirement area is the availability of good health care. In my judgment it need not be a metropolitan area with teaching and research facilities, but it should have good basic primary care.

5. Service opportunities. This includes the availability of full- or part-time work to supplement your income, to allow you to continue to support

God's cause, and to witness for and serve God personally. This consideration probably precludes living in an Adventist ghetto.

"In summary, retirement as we know it is a relatively new practice. Few people just two or three generations ago believed it was necessary to stop all activity simply because one was 62 or 65 years old. Most likely we will return to that same philosophy when most of our modern-day programs prove to be unsatisfactory and inadequate. That does not mean that you cannot plan toward a less-productive period of advanced age, but it does mean that your plans should be compatible with God's purpose for you at age 65 and beyond.

"It is interesting to note the outcome of a recent study by Harvard University. The study involved two groups of Harvard graduates between the ages of 65 and 75. One group of 100 men retired at age 65, and the other group of 100 continued to work to age 75. In the first group—those who had retired at age 65—seven out of eight were dead by age 75. In the second group—men who continued to work—only one in eight had died. The conclusion of this study was that retiring too early in life significantly reduces one's longevity in later years.

"If your goal for retirement is a life of ease, heed the warning this study provides. If your retirement goal is to continue a life of service to the Lord, perhaps unencumbered by a need for a large or steady salary, then more power to you. As Christian businessman and leader R. G. LeTourneau once said to his longtime friend Dr. Robert Barnhouse, 'Maybe I will retire someday, but I'm just too busy right now.' He was about 80 years old at the time!" (Burkett, pp. 5-7).

Remember the rich fool mentioned earlier in this chapter and note the Bible's condemnation of hoarding. We will discuss hoarding in more detail in chapter 11. Some Christians have planned too well for retirement. They have enough stored for at least three lifetimes already, and they continue to accumulate even more. Funds that could have gone to feed starving children or to assist in the Global Missions projects of the church instead wind up in a retirement account simply because it is a good tax shelter! Again, there is nothing wrong with retirement planning, but God will condemn hoarding (under any guise).

Jesus counseled those waiting for His second coming not just to watch but to continue faithful working as well. "Therefore you also be ready, for the Son of Man is coming at an hour when you do not expect Him. Who then is a faithful and wise servant, whom his master made ruler over his household, to give them food in due season? Blessed is that servant whom his master, when he comes, will find so doing" (Matthew 24:44-46).

APPLICATION
Chapter 9

1. What factors should one consider regarding when to retire?

2. Why is where one retires of great importance?

3. Why is it so critical to be debt-free—including that of your home mortgage—when you retire?

4. What contributions can retired men and women make to society and God's church?

———— ◆ ————

CHAPTER TEN

"For there is a man whose labor is with wisdom, knowledge, and skill; yet he must leave his heritage to a man who has not labored for it. This also is vanity and a great evil" (Ecclesiastes 2:21).

Inheritance and Estate Planning

Probably no subject discussed in this book is surrounded with more ignorance of God's plan than this one. At least it was the case for me. We have rewritten our entire estate plan since studying this subject from God's Word and the writings of Ellen White.

The Bible indicates in the parable of the talents in Matthew 25 and elsewhere that we will all have to give an account to God in the judgment of the way we spent the money He has entrusted to us. We render it either when we lay down this earthly life or when we meet Him at the Second Coming.

Estate planning is the crowning act of our master/servant relationship. And as I have said so many times in my seminars, "If you die without a will, the state assumes that you are an atheist, because in no case will it give any of your estate back to God through a church or charity. Should you die without a will, the state's laws of intestacy and descent and distribution come into play. In every state in the union your possessions will pass on to your relatives whether you like them or not, whether they need it or not, whether or not they would make good use of the money, and whether or not each would get the proportion of your estate that you would have wanted them to receive."

People tend to put off estate planning until they are almost too old to deal with it. In legal terms it is called "lacking capacity." Evidently some think that if they make a will, they will die sooner. It's not true, of course. You just die prepared! On the other hand, many young couples mistakenly feel that because they really have a negative net worth (student loans, car loans, etc.), they don't need a will. (I have even had young adults with children say the same thing.) From my perspective, every married person should have a will.

No one knows the time or manner of his or her death. However, we do know that unless we live to see Jesus come, we will all die. Statistically, the leading cause of death for young people is accidents. And 50 percent of the time an accident that does kill you isn't your fault. If as a young parent you die as the result of the negligent act of a third party, your estate could have a legal action in wrongful death to recover the amount you could have earned to support your family had you lived. In some cases this sum could total in the millions of dollars—quite an estate indeed.

By now your study of this book should have made it clear to you that God owns everything and that we are simply stewards of His property. Really, it all comes down to the fact that if you recognize God as the owner and your role as a steward, then if you have assets in your possession when you die, you should make provision for anyone dependent on you, but all the remaining or unused assets should be distributed in harmony with the will of God, their rightful owner. Unfortunately, this rarely happens, as we shall see.

Responsibility for Stewardship

Each of us is responsible for our own stewardship. We cannot discharge it by merely transferring our assets to others—even our relatives. If we give them to another, we make that person responsible for our stewardship, and then we become accountable for the way he or she uses the money.

Let me share with you an experience I had so you can begin making practical applications as we consider this important subject. After sharing the principles that we will discuss in this chapter with a group of people, a woman I will call Mrs. Smith said she wanted to talk with me. Here in a nutshell is her story and that of many others whom God has blessed for this time:

"Forty-seven years ago my husband and I moved from a rural area closer to a large city so that the children could attend church school and so that we could be nearer church and the conveniences of town. We purchased 50 acres of land with an old dirt road running through it. We built a house on one side of the property, and my husband farmed the rest. Three years ago he passed away, leaving me to settle our affairs. [In America 85 percent of the time the husband predeceases the wife, leaving her to take care of the property and divide the assets. Unfortunately, the wife is usually the least informed in such matters.]

"I didn't really know what to do with the property and assets, but I realized that I had to do something, so I had an attorney prepare my will in which I simply gave each of my three children one third of the assets. Now you come along and tell me that I am responsible to God for my estate planning. What should I do?"

"Well," I said, "I don't plan to tell you what you should do, but I could steer you to some principles that you could apply for yourself to your own situation.

"Let me ask you a few questions. You stated that your present plan was to divide your assets among your children. Are they still dependent on you? Are they still in school? Are they physically handicapped or institutionalized and require expensive care?"

"Oh, no," she said, "we have given them all a good education. They are professional people with nice homes and cars and so forth. I just didn't know what else to do with the money. To make matters worse," she explained, "just a few days ago a man in a business suit stopped by my home and said he would like to make an offer to buy my property. I told him it wasn't for sale, and he said that he guessed as much since he hadn't seen any signs or advertisements. But he still wanted to follow up with his company's request to make an offer on the property. Even though I repeated that I had no interest in selling at this time, he said that he just wanted to leave me his business card with the offer written on the back. I said I would take the card but still did not intend to sell.

"I guess I should tell you that the old dirt road that ran through our property when we purchased it years ago is now a four-lane highway, and that my neighbors on all four sides are shopping centers. After the man left I glanced at his card, which indicated that he represented a large retail store chain. Then I turned the card over and looked at it. This land which we had paid about $5,000 for, he was offering to buy for $250,000—*per acre!* I couldn't believe it! Quickly grabbing my purse, I took out my little calculator and entered 50 times 250,000. No, that couldn't be right. I tried it a second time and then a third. Each time it came out $12.5 million. And now you tell me that I am responsible to God for these assets. What should I do now?"

What would you tell Mrs. Smith? What would you do with the property if it was yours and you were her age with a good regular monthly income from other investments? What would God's counsel be in this matter? Does it really make any difference what she does? I hope you will discover the answers to these questions in the following pages.

Please carefully and prayerfully consider the principles outlined in this chapter. It could literally change the direction of your life. It did for me!

To establish a proper setting and foundation for what I have discovered in this area, let me share a few statistics and background information.

In this area of life you don't want to be average or normal! Let me illustrate. A decade or more ago when America was really getting serious about cholesterol and its accompanying risk of coronary heart disease, some doctors told their patients with cholesterol levels of 240-260, "Don't worry, you have normal readings." What they didn't explain to their patients was that the average or "normal" guy was at high risk for a killer chronic disease whose first symptom was often sudden death! Who wants to be normal under such circumstances?

So also in the area of estate planning, the average "normal" guy is doing it all wrong, with disastrous results. What is the average estate plan like? It's whatever the states' laws of intestacy dictate, because 80 percent of Americans still die without a will. Even worse, of those who do make a will, most of them get bad counsel and end up giving the bulk of their estates to relatives and leave God—who gave all for them—almost entirely out of their plans. Only a small percentage follow God's will in this matter.

Ellen White on Estate Planning

It has been said that the person who will not read has no advantage over the person who cannot. For all practical purposes they are both illiterate. A wealth of information on this subject awaits the Christian who wants aid in money management. Ellen White received a great deal of counsel on estate planning and spoke and wrote on it with considerable concern. God showed her that Christian's should be especially interested in having their house in order in the area of estate planning during the last days. In the balance of this chapter I will share with you some representative statements that I suggest you study for yourself in their context. For example, note the following:

"Many are going directly contrary to the light which God has given to His people, because they do not read the books which contain the light and knowledge in cautions, reproofs, and warnings" (*Testimonies,* vol. 4, p. 391).

What this says to me is that if God's way is east, many people are headed due west and don't even realize it.

"I was shown the awful fact that Satan and his angels have had more to do with the management of the property of God's professed people than the Lord has. Stewards of the last days are unwise" (*ibid.,* vol. 1, p. 199).

When writing about "wills and legacies" (*ibid.,* vol. 4, pp. 476-485), Ellen White commented, "When the judgment shall sit and the books shall be opened, every man will be rewarded according to his works. Many names are enrolled on the church book that have robbery recorded against them in the Ledger of Heaven. And unless these repent and work for the Master with disinterested benevolence, they will certainly share in the doom of the unfaithful steward" (*ibid.,* vol. 4, pp. 481, 482).

"Let it ever be kept in mind that the present selfish system of disposing of property is not God's plan, but man's device. Christians should be reformers and break up this present system, giving an entirely new aspect to the formation of wills. Let the idea be ever present that it is the Lord's property which you are handling. The will of God in this matter is law" (*ibid.,* vol. 4, pp. 482, 483).

If she says anything, it is that those who disregard God's counsel in the area of estate planning could share the fate of the unfaithful steward. However, there is an alternative—we can be reformers in this area, breaking away from the present system and giving an entirely new aspect to the way we prepare our wills. We would do this by keeping in mind that it is the Lord's property that we are handling and that His will in the matter of estate planning is divine law.

As an attorney, I frequently have Adventist clients ask my advice about drafting their will. The role of an attorney in estate planning is to assist clients in accomplishing their desires by preparing the proper documents and having them properly signed and witnessed. An attorney is not to tell the client what to do. I usually share with those that ask me this counsel: Prayerfully consider God's counsel given through His last-day prophet on this topic. Consider the statements in their context, such as the entire chapter entitled "Wills and Legacies." Then carefully examine your own personal situation and shape your plans in harmony with God's expressed will. This may require the aid of experienced and godly persons.

Is there really a plan that God has outlined for Christians to follow in managing their possessions? I believe so.

"God has devised plans that all may work intelligently in the distribution of their means. He does not propose to sustain His work by miracles. . . . The church is asleep as to the work it might do if it would give up all for Christ. A true spirit of self-sacrifice would be an argument for the reality and power of the gospel which the world could not misunderstand or gainsay, and abundant blessings would be poured upon the church" (*ibid.,* vol. 4, pp. 483, 484).

Principles of Estate Planning

I mentioned earlier what the average Christian does about estate planning. Now I'll present what I believe is God's plan. Following that, I will give the rationale and the evidence for it, but first let me state plainly the principles as I understand them.

• God is the owner of everything.

• We are stewards—managers.

• Many families go directly contrary to God's will in this regard.

• God wants us to conduct our estate planning in an entirely new and different way.

• Each person must be personally responsible in handling the assets that God has given him or her.

God says that Christian stewards have three areas on which they can legitimately spend.

1. Their own needs.
2. The needs of others.
3. Advancing God's cause.

• We should live prudently, seeking to minimize our own needs so that we can maximize our contributions to assist others and God's church.

• Always we should live within our means—avoiding debt if at all possible.

• And we have a responsibility to support those who depend on us for their needs.

• The goal of Christian parents is to train their children to become independent adults.

• When we lay down our earthly life, we should distribute our remaining assets in harmony with the will of God, the rightful owner.

• Daily we live out the parables of Matthew 25. Our very eternal life depends upon the use we make of the talents (temporal means [*ibid.,* vol. 1, p. 197]) that God has entrusted to us.

• Many of us have assets that have appreciated in value and should be liquidated and stored up in heaven before the money becomes useless.

As we noted in the last chapter, right before the end of time (in the near future) money will become worthless. Therefore we should use it in a wise manner while we still have some and can still buy and sell.

Many Christians feel that the mere mention from the pastor or other church employees of what they should do with their property is out of place. Some pastors and church leaders feel that what others do with their money is none of their business, so they hesitate to broach the subject with others.

But we are told, "Many manifest a needless delicacy on this point. They feel that they are stepping upon forbidden ground when they introduce the subject of property to the aged or to invalids in order to learn what disposition they design to make of it. But this duty is just as sacred as the duty to preach the word to save souls" (*ibid.,* vol. 4, p. 479).

Now follow four different explanations of what to do with estate planning.

"There are aged ones among us who are nearing the close of their probation; but for the want of wide-awake men to secure to the cause of God the means in their possession, it passes into the hands of those who are serving Satan. This means was only lent them of God to be returned to Him; but in nine cases out of ten these brethren, when passing from the stage of action, appropriate God's property in a way that cannot glorify Him, for not one dollar of it will ever flow into the Lord's treasury" (*ibid.,* vol. 4, p. 478).

Several facts jump out at the reader. For example, when you die, it is your personal close of probation. Fellow church members should remind you that God only lent you your possessions and you should return them to God. And by restoring His property to the Lord's treasury, we glorify Him. The next paragraph makes similar points:

"Here is a man with God's money or property in his hands. He is about to change his stewardship. Will he place the means which God has lent him to be used in His cause, in the hands of wicked men, just because they are his relatives? Should not Christian men feel interested and anxious for that man's future good as well as for the interest of God's cause, that he shall make a right disposition of his Lord's money, the talents lent him for wise improvement?" (*ibid.,* vol. 4, p. 479).

Here we again learn that the money and property belong to God, that He lent them to us to use in His service. At death we give an account of our stewardship. Accordingly, what one does in an estate plan is the crowning act of stewardship. Christians should be concerned that their fellow believers do not harm themselves and their church by wrongly disposing of their possessions. And of significant interest is the fact that Ellen White reminds us that the talents (of Matthew 25) lent us for wise improvement are the Lord's money. I will enlarge upon this in the next chapter.

The seriousness of leaving God out of our estate planning appears in the following statement. She is still talking about the same hypothetical person. "Will his brethren stand by and see him losing his hold on this life and at the same time robbing the treasury of God? This would be a fearful loss to himself and to the cause; for, by placing his talent of means in the hands of those who have no regard for the truth of God, he would, to all intents and purposes, be wrapping it in a napkin and hiding it in the earth" (*ibid.,* vol. 4, p. 479).

I gather from her statement that we should be so concerned about the eternal life of fellow believers and the church that we would be willing to speak to another in a tactful and Christian way to prevent such a terrible loss both to the person and God's mission on earth.

Last-day Estate Planning

So what new and unique plan of estate planning should last-day Christians follow? Simply stated, it is as follows:

• We should recognize that what we do with what we possess at the time of our death deserves just as important management as what we do with our possessions while we are alive.

• We should not wait until we are about to die and then think about our responsibilities.

• God would like us to be the ones that determine where our possessions go. A typical will chooses someone else to divide the maker's assets after death. Under the plan that Christians should practice, you become, in a manner of speaking, your own executor, whereby you do your best to distribute your assets yourself while you are alive. Then you can have the satisfaction of seeing the benefits and results yourself. Should you still have a portion of your possessions left when you die, you distribute them following God's outline through your will. Note how Ellen White outlines the new plan.

"The Lord would have His followers dispense their means while they can do it themselves. Some may inquire: 'Must we actually dispossess ourselves of everything which we call our own?' We may not be required to do this now; but we must be willing to do so for Christ's sake. We must acknowledge that our possessions are absolutely His, by using of them freely whenever means is needed to advance His cause" (*ibid.*).

Following the same line of reasoning, Mrs. White tells us, "That which many propose to defer until they are about to die, if they were Christians indeed they would do while they have a strong hold on life. They would devote themselves and their property to God, and, while acting as His stewards, they would have the satisfaction of doing their duty. By becoming their own executors, they could meet the claims of God themselves, instead of shifting the responsibility upon others" (*ibid.,* p. 480).

Doesn't this really make sense? If God gives you the responsibility of managing certain funds, shouldn't you do it instead of handing them over to others or letting someone you appoint do it?

What are some other advantages of being your own executor? By dispersing your own assets, others will not be able to contest the gifts as they could in typical wills. In addition, you can personally see and rejoice in the benefits that they produce. And of course, you will have the satisfaction of knowing that you are handling God's entrusted talents properly.

The example of king David and his desire to build a house for God is an excellent example of good planning. First, he did all that he could do while he was living to ensure the success of the project, and then he made proper arrangements for its completion after his death. David did not see the Temple built, but he was able to gather the precious metals, stones, and woods for its construction. Then, "seeing that his end was near, the king summoned the princes of Israel, with representative men from all parts of the kingdom, to receive this legacy in trust. He desired to commit to them his dying charge and secure their concurrence and support in the great work to be accomplished" (*Patriarchs and Prophets,* p. 750). In the past the church has done little to educate our members on the significant role their estate plan plays both in their eternal life and the success of the church itself.

Trust Services Department

That is why the church established its Trust Services Department. Years ago Ellen White told us, "Some wills are made in so loose a manner that they will not stand the test of the law, and thus thousands of dollars have been lost to the cause. Our brethren should feel that a responsibility rests upon them, as faithful servants in the cause of God, to exercise their intellect in regard to this matter, and secure to the Lord His own" (*Counsels on Stewardship,* p. 323).

Since the Seventh-day Adventist Church started following God's leading in this area, its benefit from maturing trusts has grown from less than $1 million a year in the late sixties to more than $50 million per year today! Our church has put into place one of the finest trust services departments in the world. It expects all trust services personnel to be certified and their organizations accredited to provide qualified services to our church membership. A team of certified public accountants audits the trust services departments on an annual basis. The main weakness of the system is how little the membership utilizes it. Perhaps some do not know that the local conference's trust services department will provide counsel and assistance in preparing a Christian estate plan according to their wishes and needs.

But the trust services department can't make your decisions for you. All they can do is provide education and assistance. They can encourage you to study the subject and your situation so you can make your own decision. In their efforts to avoid even the appearance of undue influence, perhaps the trust department has not educated members enough about their responsibilities to God.

From a Christian perspective, the bottom line issue that we face is how to live a prudent life so that we can minimize our own needs and maximize our contributions to God and to help others. We should do our best to utilize what God has entrusted to us in this manner, and then in the event that we are not able to give it all away before we die, our testamentary instruments (trusts and will) can provide the final settlement and distribution.

"Those who wait till death before they make a disposition of their property surrender it to death rather than to God. In so doing many are acting directly contrary to the plan of God plainly stated in His Word" (*Testimonies,* vol. 4, p. 480).

"Those who hold fast their property till the last moment surrender it to death rather than to the cause. Losses are occurring continually. Banks fail, and property is consumed in very many ways. . . . Satan works to prevent the means from coming into the treasury at all" (*ibid.,* vol. 5, p. 154).

In her statement from volume 4 of the *Testimonies,* Ellen White says that many are going directly contrary to the plan of God plainly stated in His Word. What is that plan? It is simply that each individual is responsible for his or her own stewardship. The Scriptures abound with references to this effect: Matthew 6:19, 20; 1 Timothy 6:17-19; Matthew 25:14-30; Ecclesiastes 2:21; Luke 18:18-30; 2 Corinthians 5:10.

Now I want to review something we spoke about earlier in the chapter. There I mentioned that only about 20 percent even make a will. But sadly, of those who do prepare one, many simply use them as a vehicle to pass on their possessions to their children. They give little thought that they are handling God's money and will ultimately have to give an account to Him for the use they made of it.

This discussion leads us to the next logical question. Should children receive the major portion of our estates? What if my children are not serving God and have no real financial needs?

Ellen White on Wills

Following is a brief summary of what I understand to be Mrs. White's position on the matter. Let me warn you ahead of time that it will be quite different from what most church members generally believe and practice.

Frequently people ask, "Is it true that Ellen White said that parents should not remember their children in their will?" That sounds rather harsh, doesn't it? You will be glad to learn—if you haven't already studied this subject—that Ellen White had a well-balanced and middle-of-the-road attitude toward children and estate planning.

In short, she urges that we should always remember our children as we plan our estates if (1) they are still dependent on their parents and therefore needy, (2) they have physical or other problems and thus are not able to provide for themselves, or (3) they will be more liberal with God's cause than the parents were.

But if the children are (1) unbelieving and therefore not good stewards of God, and (2) financially well off, and (3) not serving God or His church, then the parents sin against the Master by giving His money to their children.

The following statements make these points clear:

"Parents should exercise the right that God has given them. He entrusted to them the talents He would have them use to His glory. The children were not to become responsible for the talents of the father. While they have sound minds and good judgment, parents should, with prayerful consideration, and with the help of proper counselors who have experience in the truth and a knowledge of the divine will, make disposition of their property. If they have children who are afflicted or are struggling in poverty, and who will make a judicious use of means, they should be considered. But if they have unbelieving children who have an abundance of this world, and who are serving the world, they commit a sin against the Master, who has made them His stewards, by placing means in their hands merely because they are their children. God's claims are not to be lightly regarded" (*ibid.*, vol. 3, p. 121).

"Parents should have great fear in entrusting children with the talents of means that God has placed in their hands, unless they have the surest evidence that their children have a greater interest in, love for, and devotion to, the cause of God than they themselves possess, and that these children will be more earnest and zealous in forwarding the work of God, and more benevolent in carrying forward the various enterprises connected with it which call for means. But many place their means in the hands of their children, thus throwing upon them the responsibility of their own stewardship, because Satan prompts them to do it. In so doing they effectually place that means in the enemy's ranks" (*ibid.*, vol. 2, p. 655).

I realize that these passages outline principles radically different from that followed by most families today. However, I do not believe that I have taken them out of context. It was quite a revelation to me to study the subject. In fact, I could cite dozens of more statements pointing out that it is robbery of God, a great mistake, and even a terrible mistake to give His money to children who do not need it or have little or no interest in God's cause. I will share just three.

"Many parents make a great mistake in placing their property out of their hands into the hands of their children while they are themselves responsible for the use or abuse of the talent lent them of God. Neither parents nor children are made happier by this transfer of property" (*ibid.*, vol. 3, p. 122).

"Fathers who selfishly retain their means to enrich their children, and who do not see the wants of the cause of God and relieve them, make a terrible mistake. The children whom they think to bless with their means are cursed with it" (*ibid.*, vol. 3, p. 121).

"I call upon our brethren to cease their robbery of God. Some are so situated that wills must be made. But in doing this, care should be taken not to give to sons and daughters means which should flow into the treasury of God" (*ibid.*, vol. 4, p. 484).

Responsibility Toward Children
What then is our responsibility toward our children? I believe that

Christian parents owe their children three things:

1. A Christian home environment that models God's love.

2. The example of a good work ethic. We should raise our children with a willingness to work and share in life's burdens. Learning to trade their time for their employer's money should be a high priority, and it will be a benefit to both.

3. The opportunity of a good education to prepare them to take their place in society and to provide for themselves.

It is highly unlikely that parents successful in the above three points will ever have children coming to them for money. It seems to me that Christian parents should have as their goal to train their children to become independent adults.

Again Mrs. White is consistent.

"If parents, while they live, would assist their children to help themselves, it would be better than to leave them a large amount at death. Children who are left to rely principally upon their own exertions make better men and women, and are better fitted for practical life than those children who have depended upon their father's estate" (*ibid.,* vol. 3, pp. 122, 123).

Practicing What We Preach

Now, I want you to think of what you would tell the Mrs. Smith we began the chapter with. What would you do if you were in her position? Maybe it would be helpful if I would get personal here and tell you (with their permission, of course) what my parents have done, as well as what Kathy and I have done to practice what we preach.

Several years ago Mom called me from across the country and said, "Ed, Dad and I have finally decided to make our wills. We feel that we should not put this off any longer. [They had just reached their 70s and had procrastinated about it, as many do.] We just have one problem to resolve, and then we can go ahead." I have three brothers (so that makes four boys in the family). Two of us are active in our Christian experience, while the other two have chosen a different path.

"The problem," my mother said, "is that we know that we should not leave large portions of money to unbelieving grown children, but we just feel that if we give all our money to the two believing children, then the other two will become upset and say, 'If that is the way Christian parents treat their children, we don't want anything to do with God or the church.' So what should we do?"

"Mom," I replied, "I have been studying this subject a lot recently. In fact, Kathy and I have just rewritten our own wills as a result." I shared with her some of the insights in this chapter. Then I said, "I believe that you should treat all four of us the same. You have already done what God expects of you by providing us a Christian home, teaching us to work, and putting us in a position where we could get a good education if we wanted to. Now your financial responsibility has ended. We are all grown men with our own jobs and don't need your money. Why don't you just give us each $500 so that we will know that you remembered us and so that we will have some assistance to travel to your funeral if you die before Jesus comes, and then give the rest all back to God?"

"Ed, that is what I was hoping you would say," she answered. "We wanted to give some to the Voice of Prophecy, and to our local church building program, and . . ." And so I had the unique privilege of drafting my own parents' will. If they should die before Jesus comes, my "inheritance" will be $500 just like each of my brothers, and the major portion of their modest estate will advance God's mission on earth.

But now what about the family who still have children dependent upon them, children who have not reached the age of majority or who have not yet finished their education? Maybe a quick look at my estate plan would be helpful.

Right after studying this material for the first time a few years ago, I received an invitation to attend the annual international ASI convention in Calgary, Alberta. Kathy, Andrew, and Melissa joined me for the trip. As I made arrangements to fly from Atlanta to Calgary and back, it dawned on me that if our plane went down, all our immediate family would lose their lives in a common accident. What would then happen to our estate?

My will was written in such a way, as many are, that if we all perished in a common accident, I was to be the one presumed to have died last and therefore my estate would contain all the family assets. And just what were they under these circumstances? Well, for starters, I had purchased the tickets with my American Express card. For a small fee it insures each ticketed person with a death benefit of $500,000. Also the travel agency gave a $100,000 life insurance policy to each person who purchased their tickets through them. So with four people thus insured for $600,000 each, that would make the total estate worth at least $2.4 million. Added to that would be my personal possessions.

Then I thought, *What would happen to our estate in the event we all died together?* At the time my will stipulated that 20 percent would return to God through the church. When I had prepared it, I had thought to myself, *God should be thrilled. After all, I am giving Him a double tithe.* (That was before I realized that it was all really His and should go back to Him when I have no further need of it.) Then we had lined up our parents and all our brothers and sisters to get the remaining 80 percent. Now we realized that we needed that entirely new aspect to our wills that would better reflect what we knew was God's plan for us.

So we changed our wills! Now our parents, should they survive us, will receive (each set) 10 percent of our estate, since they took care of us when we were young and may need us when they are older. The 80 percent balance returns to God, its rightful owner, by way of His church. And what about our siblings? They are all adults with their own lives to live. God has not made them responsible for our stewardship, so we must perform it as He directs.

Now, quickly, two short scenarios. What happens if Kathy and I both die and leave dependent children? We have made provision for an educational trust fund so that our children will be able to complete their education and therefore enter the job market with enough training to be successful. In addition, we will leave them a token amount as a love gift, but the bulk of our estate will aid God's work.

A couple years ago when Andrew returned home from college for Christmas break, I asked him how he was enjoying school. He answered that he guessed things were going pretty well, since he was enjoying school and doing fine in his classes. "I am glad to hear that," I said, "because you are now spending your inheritance." We had covered the topic together several times before, so he knew that his mother and I would do our best to make sure that, with his work assistance and our support, he would graduate from college without any student loans, have a car paid for, and have acquired some work experience that would do him well for the future. After that, we would turn our support to the church we love and to the God who had died for us.

The Time of Trouble

One final observation. You have heard about the following passage before, but maybe not in this context. Please note carefully what Ellen White says about praying for the sick near the end of time:

"[God] knows whether or not those for whom petitions are offered would be able to endure the trial and test that would come upon them if they lived. He knows the end from the beginning. Many will be laid away to sleep before the fiery ordeal of the time of trouble shall come upon our world. This is another reason why we should say after our earnest petitions; 'Nevertheless not my will, but thine, be done' (Luke 22:42). Such a petition will never be registered in heaven as a faithless prayer" (*Counsels on Health, p. 375*).

Now you see the picture more clearly. God in His great wisdom and mercy will allow those who are older or more feeble to rest from their labors during the time of trouble. It will relieve them of this terrible ordeal as well as the stress of those who would have to look after them and care for them. But remember also that this older generation has the highly appreciated assets. If properly counseled, they could leave these assets to God through His church to help finance the world's evangelization.

In a letter to Gilbert Collins (dated January 3, 1902) Ellen White told him, "My brother, you may not live long. Have you made your will? We know that you want to be the Lord's right hand, working in cooperation with Him. Even after your life ends, it is your privilege to carry forward His work. Will you please consider this, and return to the Lord His own, that you may know that you have faithfully acted your part, doing what you could? If you do this, when you are called to lay off your armor, you will illustrate the words that God instructed John to write: 'Blessed are the dead which die in the Lord from henceforth: yea, saith the Spirit, that they may rest from their labors; and their works do follow them' (Rev. 14:13)" (*Manuscript Releases,* vol. 4, pp. 320, 321).

According to her interpretation, the works that follow the righteous dead are the good things done with the money they return to God through their wills when they die. What will heaven say about us? Can we claim the promise of Revelation 14:13 based on our present estate plan? Obviously we could say much more about this subject, but perhaps this overview is sufficient. Please remember that it is up to you to handle the money God has put in your possession. I pray that for your sake and that of God's cause you will become your own executor and return to God all you can while you are alive, and then in the final accounting, the crowning act of your stewardship, you will again be faithful to your charge.

APPLICATION
Chapter 10

1. God has a claim on all our possessions by virtue of creation and redemption. How will recognizing this fact affect our estate planning?

2. What is the entirely new concept of Christian wills that Ellen White suggests?

3. Take the time to look over your present estate documents and compare them with God's counsel. If you do not have a Christian estate plan, set aside time to prepare this important part of your money management strategy.

4. Is there some course of action that you could follow now to become your own executor and utilize some of your surplus blessings to help others and assist in God's cause?

---◆---

"Do not lay up for yourselves treasures on earth, where moth and rust destroy and where thieves break in and steal; but lay up for yourselves treasures in heaven, where neither moth nor rust destroys and where thieves do not break in and steal" (Matthew 6:19, 20).

Worry-free Investments

People frequently ask me where they should invest their money. In today's economy they are not as worried about their rate of return as they are about the safety of the principal amount.

Do you know any safe place to keep money? I don't! At least not on this earth. When we talk about investing, the big question is What is the level of risk that you are willing to live with? The choices range from the low-interest and low-risk government-backed securities to the high-yield and high-risk commodities market.

I would like to begin this chapter with a short philosophy statement and then flesh out its concepts in the balance of the chapter. Let's first ask a few questions. Where do investment funds come from, anyway? What is the purpose of investing? Why not spend the money now? Are there positive benefits to investing? Can one really invest without any risk at all, as some suggest? What is the difference between saving and investing? Is investing the same as hoarding?

What Are Investment Funds?

Investment funds are those moneys that we do not need for our regular personal expenses. It is the surplus of funds that God promises to the faithful tither. God says, "'Bring all the tithes into the storehouse, that there may be food in My house, and prove Me now in this,' says the Lord of hosts, 'if I will not open for you the windows of heaven and pour out for you such blessing that there will not be room enough to receive it'" (Malachi 3:10).

If we don't have room enough to receive it, then we have more than we need—a surplus. It is from such surplus funds that Christians make investments. And also from them we can store up treasures in heaven.

One could simply take such extra money and put it in a shoe box under the bed or in a waterproof container buried in the backyard. Or an individual could rent a safe-deposit box at a bank and simply keep the extra money there. The major problem with such surplus money management is that it is not really investing. Obviously questions will arise about the safety of money under the bed or in the backyard, or even in the bank, for that matter. But safety questions still do not define investing. Investing is putting one's money "to work." While it works, it returns to the investor either a dividend or interest or both. A bad investment could, of course, produce neither, and might even erode part or all of the funds invested.

People typically use investments to enhance present income, save up money for retirement, or simply increase net worth. Some actually employ their investments for their entire income or living. Others use the proceeds from investments to support worthy causes. It is my observation that many low- to middle-income families do not actually have much in the way of cash investments. They invest in education for themselves or their children and in the real estate they are purchasing.

The types of investing described above always have some risk. The risk involves the amount of interest one may receive and the safety of the invested money itself—the capital. That is, the investment may not "perform" as the investor had hoped. In addition, in some kinds of investments (the stock market, for example), one could actually lose part or all of the capital, or investment money.

Family Savings

Generally, financial advisers suggest that a family's basic savings account for unexpected or emergency spending should be the equivalent of three to six months' income. This would cover such things as car problems, replacing major appliances, or repairing or replacing the water or heating system in your home. Further, it is a good plan to have a savings account to purchase the next automobile for cash. People also save for their children's college education. Our plan in this regard has been to emphasize debt-free living so that by the time the children are ready for college, you will have the home as well as other debts paid off, thereby freeing the monthly income that went to these other debts for school tuition, retirement needs, helping others, and contributing to God.

Before we look further at savings and investments, let me mention just briefly that some who read this book will find themselves tempted to say, "Why don't authors talk to average people when they write books on finances? We don't have any money to invest. And most of those we know don't either." One of the main points of this book is to help its readers realize that with proper management all can save something for future needs. Many families find that their needs seem to grow to meet the level of their income no matter how much they earn. Others discover that they are so far in debt that it takes all they make to keep the wolf away from the door. How could a family ever save anything under those circumstances?

"I have known a family receiving twenty dollars a week to spend every penny of this amount, while another family of the same size, receiving but twelve dollars a week, laid aside one or two dollars a week, managing to do this by refraining from purchasing things which seemed to be necessary but which could be dispensed with" (*The Adventist Home,* p. 396).

Saving for future needs and hoarding are not the same. Both Scripture and Ellen White encourage setting aside money for emergencies or to make contributions to God's cause. However, simply saving for financial security becomes hoarding, and Inspiration discourages it. Note the counsel from 1 Timothy 6:6-19.

"But godliness with contentment is great gain. For we brought nothing into this world, and it is certain we can carry nothing out. And having food and clothing, with these we shall be content. But those who desire to be rich fall into temptation and a snare, and into many foolish and harmful lusts which drown men in destruction and perdition. For the love of money is a root of all kinds of evil, for which some have strayed from the faith in their greediness, and pierced themselves through with many sorrows. But you, O man of God, flee these things and pursue righteousness, godliness, faith, love, patience, gentleness. Fight the good fight of faith, lay hold on eternal life, to which you were also called and have confessed the good confession in the presence of many witnesses. . . . Command those who are rich in this present age not to be haughty, nor to trust in uncertain riches but in the living God, who gives us richly all things to enjoy. Let them do good, that they be rich in good works, ready to give, willing to share, storing up for themselves a good foundation for the time to come, that they may lay hold on eternal life."

Treasures in Heaven

If you are really seeking the will of God in your financial management, several questions immediately come to mind when we think about savings or investments. Jesus Himself said right in the middle of the Sermon on the Mount: "Do not lay up for yourselves treasures on earth" (Matthew 6:19). And I have to ask myself what He means by that. Then we need to remember Jesus' encounter with the rich young ruler. After the Jewish leader recited to Jesus the details of his life of obedience to the commandments, Jesus said to him, "You still lack one thing. Sell all that you have and distribute to the poor, and you will have treasure in heaven; and come, follow Me" (Luke 18:22).

When He commissioned the disciples, He told them, "Provide neither gold nor silver nor copper in your moneybelts, nor bag for your journey, nor two tunics, nor sandals, nor staffs; for a worker is worthy of his food" (Matthew 10:9, 10). Again Matthew states in essence in chapter 6, "Don't worry about what you will eat, drink, or wear. God knows you need these things. If you put His kingdom first, these things will be provided for you."

And in addition, we have the story of the rich fool. The man had received such blessings on his business that he said to himself, "Soul, you have many goods laid up for many years; take your ease; eat, drink, and be merry" (Luke 12:19). Because his personal needs were cared for, he thought he could just stop working and live to please himself. You know the result of that decision.

Do these things apply to us, or just to a bygone era? Should one spend all extra money only on others and God's cause? Is there any balancing counsel in God's revealed will? I believe that there is. Over and over Scripture and the writings of Ellen White remind us that there are legitimate uses for money. Usually Inspiration keeps repeating three need areas. The following is a representative statement. "Money has great value, because it can do great good. . . . But money is of no more value than sand, only as it is put to use in providing for the necessities of life, in blessing others, and advancing the cause of Christ" (*Christ's Object Lessons,* p. 351).

Note that God always puts our need first. Then He invites us to look at the possibility of helping others and making contributions to advance His cause. Evidently God tests us by letting us go first to see whether we will use it all on ourselves or will share with others.

Assuming, as we noted above in Malachi 3:10, that God wants us to have a surplus of funds, the question then is what do good stewards do with them. Fortunately, we have some answers. "You might today have had a capital of means to use in case of emergency and to aid the cause of God, if you had economized as you should. Every week a portion of your wages should be reserved and in no case touched unless suffering actual want, or to render back to the Giver in offerings to God" (*The Adventist Home,* pp. 395, 396).

"The rules from God's Word about investing still work. Apply them and you will prosper over the long run. Violate them, and you will lose all that you have worked so hard to accumulate" (Larry Burkett, *Investing for the Future,* pp. 8, 9).

The bottom line on investments seems to me to be not whether or not we save money, but rather why we save it and how much we save. As we have noted above, there are three good uses of money: to provide for our own needs, to help others, and to further God's mission on earth. The "why" of savings is easier to address than the "how much." Obviously, the "how much" would depend on individual circumstances. For example, those anticipating retirement because of physical limitations at some time in the future would not need large savings if they are debt-free, including that of their home. They could live quite well if they have Social Security and a company retirement plan with continuing health insurance. On the other hand, if they need to supplement Social Security, then they must have some other source of income, such as investments.

Motives for Saving

The "why" or motive for saving centers on three major reasons: (1) to set aside for our own future needs both in the area of emergencies as well as known expenses (such as the purchase of a car or educating our children); (2) to assist others in need; and (3) to further the gospel. The biblical perspective recognizes only these three legitimate reasons, as we clearly see demonstrated in the three parables of Matthew 25 (which we will discuss in more detail in the next chapter).

Where should one start when planning investments? In the first area of personal needs, a family should invest in debt reduction and in their own home mortgage. (It is understood that we should also contribute to the second and third categories at the same time.) Other financial experts agree on the need for home and debt reduction.

"It is my strong conviction that becoming debt-free, including the home mortgage, should be the first investment goal for any young couple (or person). Once you have achieved that goal, then, and only then, should you invest in other areas" (Burkett, p. 142).

Ellen White states this preference and order as well. "Had Brother and Sister B been economical managers, denying themselves, they could ere this have had a home of their own and besides this have had means to draw upon in case of adversity" (*The Adventist Home,* p. 395).

Financial experts tell us that the average American is only three weeks away from bankruptcy. Many have little or no money saved, face major monthly credit obligations, and totally depend on the next paycheck to keep the budget afloat.

The Bible encourages us to set aside reserve funds. "The wise man saves for the future, but the foolish man spends whatever he gets" (Proverbs 21:20, TLB.) The opposite of debt, saving will make provision for the future while debt presumes upon the future.

Hoarding

On the other hand, Inspiration discourages hoarding, which we have defined as saving for financial security. Hoarding could cause serious problems in the future. I see at least four major problems with hoarding money—saving beyond our personal, basic needs.

First, in a failed economy, one could lose all he has saved (hoarded). By now you are surely aware that the United States economy is in a precarious position. Many people don't recognize that our country doesn't have enough money actually printed to pay everyone off in cash. In the event that each person actually wanted to hold all the money that he or she "owned," there would not be enough physical bills or notes to meet the demand. Only 20 percent, or one fifth, of the U.S. monetary system is actually cash. Eighty percent, or four fifths, of our "money" is really only data on bank computer records.

We all know now that it is possible to lose our "paper" investments overnight, for example, in the event of a stock market collapse. Let's note some of Ellen White's counsel in this area.

"The very means that is now so sparingly invested in the cause of God, and that is selfishly retained, will in a little while be cast with all idols to the moles and to the bats. Money will soon depreciate in value very suddenly when the reality of eternal scenes opens to the senses of man.

"God will have men who will venture anything and everything to save souls" (*Evangelism,* p. 63).

"It is a snare of the last days to involve God's people in loss of their Lord's entrusted capital, that should be used wisely in the work of winning souls" (*Counsels on Stewardship,* p. 243).

"Those who hold fast their property till the last moment surrender it to death rather than to the cause. Losses are occurring continually. Banks fail, and property is consumed in very many ways. . . . Satan works to prevent the means from coming into the treasury at all" (*Testimonies,* vol. 5, p. 154).

The second problem with hoarding is that some will hold on to their money so long that it cannot be used to benefit the cause of God.

While doing the research for this section I found what to me was a most sobering section of material from Ellen White's pen. In *Testimonies,* volume 1, pages 170 and following, she wrote about the rich young ruler. I will share here only that portion most relevant to the topic at hand. "Here is the reward for those who sacrifice for God. They receive a hundredfold in this life, and shall inherit everlasting life. . . . Those who still cling to their earthly treasure, and will not make a right disposition of that which is lent them of God, will lose their treasure in heaven, lose everlasting life. . . . The work is closing; and soon the means of those who have kept their riches, their large farms, their cattle, etc., will not be wanted. I saw the Lord turn to such in anger, in wrath, and repeat these words: 'Go to now, ye rich men" (James 5:1, KJV). He has called, but you would not hear. Love of this world has drowned His voice. Now He has no use for you, and lets you go, bidding you: 'Go to now, ye rich men.'

"Oh, I saw that it was an awful thing to be thus forsaken by the Lord—a fearful thing to hold onto a perishable substance here, when He has said that if we will sell and give alms, we can lay up treasure in heaven. I was shown that as the work is closing up, and the truth is going forth in mighty power, these rich men will bring their means and lay it at the feet of the servants of God, begging them to accept it. The answer from the servants of God will be: 'Go to now, ye rich men. Your means is not needed. Ye withheld it when ye could do good with it in advancing the cause of God. The needy have suffered; they have not been blessed by your means. God will not accept your riches now. Go to now, ye rich men'" (pp. 173-175).

This statement is awesome in its power, boldness, and implications. It does not really need any interpretation by me. I will close this section with just one more reference.

"Now is the time for all to work. . . . What will many answer in the day of God, when He inquires, What have ye done for Me, who gave My riches, My honor, My command, and My life to save you from ruin? The do-nothings will be speechless in that day. They will see the sin of their neglect. They have robbed God of the service of a lifetime. They have not influenced any for good. They have not brought one soul to Jesus. They felt content to do nothing for the Master; and they meet no reward, but eternal loss. They perish with the wicked, although they professed to be followers of Christ" (*Counsels on Stewardship,* pp. 123, 124).

The third problem with hoarding money appears in the Revelation 13:17 scenario. Perhaps I can illustrate it this way. You have $300,000 invested in mutual funds and can live comfortably on the interest. Then end-time events begin to unfold, and the authorities declare that no one can buy or sell without receiving the mark of the beast. In other words, your money that you have worked so hard to save and now depend upon to take care of you is worthless unless you accept the religious authority of the state. What are you going to do? Are you willing to turn your back on your $300,000 and walk away? After all, that amount represents 30 years' worth of house payments! That is why Jesus said, "Remember Lot's wife" (Luke 17:32).

It boils down to the question "Do I want to be able to spend my hard-earned money, or give it up, depend entirely on the providence of God, and maybe even lose my life as a result?" The sad part is that many Christians with hoarded assets will go for the money and turn their backs on God and eternal life. And then to add insult to injury, they will lose it all in a few months or weeks anyway, just as everyone else does. Also they will forfeit their eternal life. "For what will it profit a man if he gains the whole world, and loses his own soul? Or what will a man give in exchange for his soul?" (Mark 8:36, 37).

"Very few realize the strength of their love for money until the test is brought to bear upon them. Many who profess to be Christ's followers then show that they are unprepared for heaven. Their works testify that they love wealth more than their neighbor or their God. Like the rich young man, they inquire the way of life; but when it is pointed out and the cost estimated, and they see that the sacrifice of earthly riches is demanded, they decide that heaven costs too much. The greater the treasures laid up on the earth, the more difficult it is for the possessor to realize that they are not his own, but are lent him to be used to God's glory" (*ibid.,* p. 150).

The fourth problem with hoarding is that our savings will testify of our selfishness and speak against us in the judgment. "Come now, you rich, weep and howl for your miseries that are coming upon you! Your riches are corrupted, and your garments are moth-eaten. Your gold and silver are corroded, and their corrosion *will be a witness against you* and will eat your flesh like fire. You have heaped up treasure in the last days" (James 5:1-3; italics supplied).

None of us would ever leave money in a bank without first opening an account and securing a receipt for each deposit. Our passbook or statement is then the official evidence of our funds actually being in the account. Ellen White suggests that our money will either testify that we have invested for eternity in heaven or document our personal selfishness.

"Hoarded wealth is not merely useless, it is a curse. In this life it is a snare to the soul, drawing the affections away from the heavenly treasure. In the great day of God its witness to unused talents and neglected opportunities will condemn its possessor" (*Christ's Object Lessons,* p. 352).

This is not just another book about money management. As I have mentioned earlier, I have felt compelled to tell what I have learned about money management from what I have studied in Scripture, Ellen White, and other Christian authors. To me this book's greatest contribution is the money management principles that we as committed Christians should follow during the last days of earth's history.

Now I want to share with you the perspective I have developed toward investing for our own future well-being, as well as God's promises to those willing to share with others and aid God's cause.

My first suggestion would be our own church's revolving fund accessed through the local conference's Trust Services Department. Someday, of course, all financial institutions will fail. But I would rather lose my money with the church than with the world. In addition, if I die without needing the money, then I can provide for the work of God to go forward.

Making Good Investments

Before going further into my suggestions for investments, I must tell you that if we ranked all 250 million Americans according to their investment knowledge and experience, millions of people would stand in line ahead of me. With this disclaimer in mind, what I will share with you now comes from others far better qualified in this area. The most comprehensive investment counsel from a Christian perspective that I am aware of is Larry Burkett's recent book, *Investing for the Future.* Chapter 5, "The Investment Hall of Horrors," and chapter 6, "The Best Investments," give the following suggestions. First, we must avoid the worst investments. Involving great risk, they have poor track records and cannot be recommended. They include commodities speculation, partnerships, tax shelters, precious metals, gemstones, coins, and stocks. On the other hand, you can, with proper guidance, find investments that will have lower risk and a better track record. Your home, mutual funds, and government-backed securities fall in this area. With the precarious state of the economy, you should consider even these only on expert advice. For example, if you invest in your home, make sure that it is in a desirable location, is well constructed, and is a good deal at the time of purchase.

One other area that we need to cover is get-rich-quick schemes. We can summarize them quickly: "(1) Don't get involved with things you don't understand. (2) Don't risk money you can't afford to lose. And (3) don't make a quick decision. The vast majority of get-rich-quick schemes are built on a pyramid base. This means they require an ever-expanding supply of new investors (suckers) in order to sustain them. Usually those who join are given a monetary incentive to sell others on the scheme. . . . These incentives employ the most innocuous of terms, such as 'finder's fees,' 'royalties,' and 'bonuses.' The bottom line is simple: If you are dumb enough to risk your hard-earned money, you must know several people who are dumber than you are" (*Investing for the Future,* pp. 52-54).

(For more information, I recommend that you purchase Larry Burkett's *Investing for the Future.* It is available at most Christian bookstores, including Adventist Book Centers.)

Spiritual Consequences of Investing

What I have discussed above is what one can do with the portion of funds a person will need for his or her own support. To conclude this chapter, I want to share with you some things Ellen White wrote to God's children in the last days. They deal with the spiritual and eternal consequences of investing. I would encourage you to study them in their context to grasp their true importance.

"Satan is pleased to have you increase your farms and invest your means in worldly enterprises, for by so doing you not only hinder the cause from advancing, but by anxiety and overwork lessen your prospect for eternal life" (*Testimonies,* vol. 5, p. 152).

I have mentioned several times in this book that the times we live in demand a new dimension and urgency toward good money management. Mrs. White tells us, "It is a snare of the last days to involve God's people in loss of their Lord's entrusted capital, that should be used wisely in the work of winning souls" (*Counsels on Stewardship,* p. 243).

Just how much of our surplus should we give to God in the last days? The answer is simple and reasonable. "Brethren, awake from your life of selfishness, and act like consistent Christians. The Lord requires you to economize your means and let every dollar not needed for your comfort flow into the treasury" (*Testimonies,* vol. 5, p. 156).

Since I have never seen this material widely published, I feel compelled to share it here. Many times when Ellen White spoke about proper money management and the needs in God's cause, her message would so move her listeners that they would ask her if they should sell their homes and place the money in the Lord's treasury. She always told them that God may not need their homes now, but that they should be laid on the altar and the Lord would impress them as to the right time to sell. She did say, however, that those with more than one property should liquidate the extra and give the money to God. Consider the following two short examples.

"God calls upon those who have possessions in lands and houses to sell and to invest the money where it will be supplying the great want in the missionary field" (*Testimonies,* vol. 5, p. 733).

"It is now that our brethren should be cutting down their possessions instead of increasing them. We are about to move to a better country, even a heavenly. Then let us not be dwellers upon the earth, but be getting things into as compact a compass as possible" (*ibid.,* vol. 5, p. 152).

We all, as a matter of course, thank God for our blessings. But have we ever thought about why He gives them to us? "If we have prosperity in our secular business, it is because God blesses us. A part of this income is to be devoted to the poor, and a large portion to be applied to the cause of God" (*ibid.,* vol. 4, p. 477).

The Safest Investment of All

We started this chapter talking about the safety of our investments. I have concluded that there is no safe place to keep money in this world. But what about the safety of what we invest in helping others and God's work?

"In giving to the work of God, you are laying up for yourselves treasures in heaven. All that you lay up is secure from disaster and loss, and is increasing to an eternal, an enduring substance" (*Counsels on Stewardship*, p. 342).

"Those who really feel an interest in the cause of God, and are willing to venture something for its advancement, will find it a sure and safe investment" (*Testimonies,* vol. 1, p. 226).

"We are to place in the Lord's treasury all the means that we can spare. For this means, needy unworked fields are calling. . . . The money invested in this work will bring rich returns" (*ibid.,* vol. 9, p. 49).

Perhaps the most interesting statement Mrs. White made about investments went to a man who had failed to make good investments and had lived primarily to please himself. She told him, "The enterprise of securing eternal life did not awaken your interest. Here you could have expended means, and run no risks, met no disappointments, and in the end would have received immense profits" (*ibid.,* vol. 2, p. 280). It sounds almost too good to be true. No risk, no disappointments, and immense profits. What an investment!

How important is our investment strategy?

"By investing their means in the cause of God to aid in the salvation of souls, and by relieving the needy, they become rich in good works, and are 'laying up in store for themselves a good foundation against the time to come, that they may lay hold on eternal life' (1 Timothy 6:19, KJV). This will prove a safe investment" (*Counsels on Stewardship*, p. 151).

"This work of transferring your possessions to the world above is worthy of all your best energies. It is of the highest importance, and involves your eternal interests" (*ibid.,* p. 342).

It may be that you don't feel that you have a surplus and therefore cannot join with those laying up treasure in heaven. But one of the primary reasons I wrote this book is to point out that with proper planning we can live within our means and faithfully support God's mission on earth.

"We can every one of us do something, if we will only take the position that God would have us. Every move that you make to enlighten others brings you nearer in harmony with the God of heaven. If you sit down and look at yourself and say, 'I can barely support my family,' you will never do anything; but if you say, 'I will do something for the truth, I will see it advance, I will do what I can,' God will open ways so that you can do something. You should invest in the cause of truth so that you will feel that you are a part of it" (*ibid.,* p. 304).

May God bless you as you seek His wisdom and blessing on your investments.

APPLICATION
Chapter 11

1. Every family should have some money in savings. How much should be in that account, and under what circumstances should the money be utilized?

2. What is the difference between savings, which is encouraged, and hoarding, which is discouraged?

3. From a scriptural and eschatological perspective, what four potential problems could develop because of hoarding?

4. How safe is money that we invest in others and in God?

◆

CHAPTER TWELVE

"For the kingdom of heaven is like a man traveling to a far country, who called his own servants and delivered his goods to them. . . . After a long time the lord of those servants came and settled accounts with them" (Matthew 25:14-19).

The Judgment Bar of God

D eep down in our hearts we all know that sooner or later we must all stand before the judgment bar of God and give an account of what we have done in our lives. Although we are saved by faith, we receive our rewards according to our actions. God longs for us to be faithful to His commands. He Himself gives us the power to be faithful, but we must receive and utilize it. In this very real sense we demonstrate the genuineness of our profession of faith, genuineness that Jesus spoke about when He said, "by their fruits you will know them" (Matthew 7:20) and "Why do you call Me 'Lord, Lord,' and do not the things which I say?" (Luke 6:46).

It is in this setting that both Matthew and Luke tell the story of the two builders. Our obedience tells God that we love and trust Him. On the other hand, our disobedience indicates that though we say that we love Him, we still want to do things our own way. Now, after reading this book to this point and learning God's desire for us in personal money management, we must decide whether or not we will order our lives in harmony with His will. Are you prepared to seek God's leading in money management and then by His grace structure your life in harmony with it?

Remember the words of Jesus. "Therefore whoever hears these sayings of Mine, and does them, I will liken him to a wise man who built his house on the rock: and the rain descended, the floods came, and the winds blew and beat on that house; and it did not fall, for it was founded on the rock. Now everyone who hears these sayings of Mine, and does not do them, will be like a foolish man who built his house on the sand: and the rain descended, the floods came, and the winds blew and beat on that house, and it fell. And great was its fall" (Matthew 7:24-27).

Money Management and End Times

In the introduction and throughout this book I have mentioned the eschatological significance of money management. Now as the capstone I will share with you what I perceive to be the connection between our personal money management and our Christian experience and preparation for end-time events.

Matthew, Mark, and Luke all record the story of the private conversation between Jesus and His disciples where they asked about the signs of the end of time (Matthew 24; 25; Mark 13; and Luke 21). We all recognize the incident's special significance for our day. When the disciples asked Him, "What will be the sign of Your coming, and of the end of the age?" (Matthew 24:3), Jesus answered:

"And there will be signs in the sun, in the moon, and in the stars; and on the earth distress of nations, with perplexity, the sea and the waves roaring; men's hearts failing them from fear and the expectation of those things which are coming on the earth, for the powers of heaven will be shaken. Then they will see the Son of Man coming in a cloud with power and great glory" (Luke 21:25-27).

Jesus here speaks not only of distress of nations, but also of perplexity. A closer look at this word, "perplexity," will point out more clearly that He was describing our day. "Perplexity" appears nowhere else in the New Testament. The Greek word was *aporia*. Lexicographers state that it literally means "without a passage out."

So the picture Jesus paints of the days just before He returns reveals a stressed world faced with apparently insurmountable problems. Ellen White describes the end-time conditions in this way: "There are not many, even among educators and statesmen, who comprehend the causes that underlie the present state of society. Those who hold the reins of government are not able to solve the problem of moral corruption, poverty, pauperism, and increasing crime. *They are struggling in vain to place business operations on a more secure basis.* If men would give more heed to the teaching of God's Word, they would find a solution of the problems that perplex them" (*Testimonies,* vol. 9, p. 13; italics supplied).

Because many recognize that our present economic problems are hopeless, we have organizations like the First American Monetary Consultants marketing materials entitled "Understanding and Avoiding the Coming Economic Wipeout." Larry Burkett states in his best-selling *The Coming Economic Earthquake,* "Eventually the majority of households will reach the stage where they cannot repay what they owe, nor will they be able to borrow more. At that point, the economy must stop while the debt is either repudiated (by a depression), devalued (by hyperinflation), or repaid (unthinkable)" (p. 106).

"By 1996, at the current rate of deficit, it will take all of the taxes paid by all taxpayers to pay the interest on the national debt. The federal government will be spending money at the rate of approximately $7 billion per minute!" (Burkett, *Investing, for the Future,* pp. 20, 21).

From both the perspective of the family and the federal government there appears to be no way out. So what can you do to protect yourself? The simple answer has appeared over and over in this book—stay or get out of debt and trust God to provide for your needs.

We have just looked at the world conditions that Jesus foretold that would exist just before His return. However, He didn't stop there. He went on to describe what things would be like in the church at the end of time. And this is what should concern each of us at the moment.

The Three Parables of Matthew 25

As part of Jesus' answer to the disciples' question, He told the three parables of Matthew 25. All of which end with the Second Coming of Jesus. The parable of the ten virgins emphasizes the importance of being ready for the Second Advent. The parable of the talents tells us what we should be doing while we wait. And the parable of the sheep and the goats lets us know the basis upon which God metes out the judgment.

I will enlarge a little on each of the stories from a money management perspective by first pointing out that each one not only depicts God's people at His coming but also parallels the uses of money that we talked about in recent chapters. Note the following parallels:

The story of the ten virgins = our needs.

The story of the talents = the advancement of God's cause.

The story of the sheep and the goats = the needs of others.

Here we see the Bible's emphasis on the three areas of appropriate money investment. Ellen White, as we have seen earlier, draws the same conclusion. "The very best legacy which parents can leave their children is a knowledge of useful labor and the example of a life characterized by disinterested benevolence. By such a life they show the true value of money, that it is only to be appreciated for the good that it will accomplish in [1] relieving their own wants, and [2] the necessities of others, and in [3] advancing the cause of God" (*Testimonies,* vol. 3, p. 399).

Parable of the Ten Virgins

Now let's take a brief look at each story to determine its application to the themes of this book. Speaking of the parable of the ten virgins, Ellen White tells us, "Those who profess to be waiting for the coming of Christ are represented in the parable by the five wise and the five foolish virgins. . . . Many profess to be wise; but have they the Holy Spirit? As a people, we profess to know the truth, but of what avail will this be if we do not carry out its principles in our life? . . . It is your business to be ready for the coming of the Lord, and you cannot be ready while failing to carry out His commands. There are some who seem to feel no responsibility concerning paying their tithes into the treasury of the Lord. They withhold from Him who has given them everything else the small portion He has named as His own" (*Signs of the Times,* Aug. 1, 1892).

Clearly anyone who does not faithfully bring his or her tithes is not ready to meet God. According to Acts 5:32, God gives the Holy Spirit, which was in short supply in the lives of the foolish virgins, to those who obey Him.

Parable of the Talents

Matthew 25 has no parallel. In other words, none of the other Gospel writers record the three stories. However, Luke 19 does have a story similar to the parable of the talents—the story of the ten minas. In it a nobleman summons 10 of his servants and gives each of them a mina—a unit currently worth thousands. In Luke 19:13 the nobleman instructs the 10 servants, "Do business till I come." The New International Version says, "Put this money to work until I come back."

What are the talents that God is talking about in this story? How does one invest them so that heaven will account a person faithful when Christ returns? It occurs to me that since the parables all are set at the end-time, the judgment, and the second coming of Christ, then their primary application must be the final generation of Christians. (Of course, they also apply to each person as life is closed.) Ellen White gives some additional insights into the parable.

"I was shown that the parable of the talents has not been fully understood. This important lesson was given to the disciples for the benefit of Christians living in the last days. And these talents do not represent merely the ability to preach and instruct from the Word of God. *The parable applies to the temporal means which God has entrusted to His people.* Those to whom the five and the two talents were given traded and doubled that which was committed to their trust. God requires those who have possessions here to put their money out to usury for Him—to put it into the cause to spread the truth" (*Testimonies,* vol. 1, p. 197; italics supplied).

So far we know that the talents represent the temporal means—money—that God has entrusted to us. And then He asks us to invest it in building up His kingdom. So what is the return on the investment? How can one know whether or not he or she is a faithful servant? *"Every soul saved is a talent gained.* If truly converted, the one brought to a knowledge of the truth will, in his turn, use the talents of influence and of means which God has given him, in working for the salvation of his fellow men" (*ibid.,* vol. 2,

p. 660; italics supplied).

"The Lord designs that the means entrusted to us shall be used in building up His kingdom. His goods are committed to His stewards that they may be carefully traded upon and bring back a revenue to Him in the saving of souls unto eternal life" (*ibid.*, vol. 6, p. 448).

I guess we all tend to think that the other person has more talents than we have and is therefore more responsible to God. In the story, however, it was the person with only one talent—the least money—that proved unfaithful.

"The one to whom is entrusted one talent is not responsible for five, or for two, but for the one. Many neglect to lay up for themselves a treasure in heaven by doing good with the means that God has lent them. They distrust God and have a thousand fears in regard to the future. Like the children of Israel they have evil hearts of unbelief " (*ibid.*, vol. 2, p. 656).

"I saw that some of God's professed people are like the man who hid his talent in the earth. They keep their possessions from doing good in the cause of God. They claim that these are their own, and that they have a right to do what they please with their own; and souls are not saved by judicious efforts made by them with their Lord's money" (*ibid.*, vol. 1, p. 198).

Several times earlier in the book we discussed the concept that God owns everything. Accordingly, the funds that He has entrusted to us we hold in a master/servant relationship to God. Simply stated, then, once we have met our needs, we are to utilize God's money for His benefit and return the entire amount—principal and interest—to Him when we are done with it.

"The Lord requires that those to whom He has lent talents of means make a right use of them, having the advancement of His cause prominent. Every other consideration should be inferior to this" (*ibid.*, vol. 2, p. 659).

"When the Master comes, the faithful servant is prepared to return Him both principal and interest. By his fruits he can show the increase of talents that he has gained to return to the Master. The faithful servant will then have done his work, and the Master, whose reward is with Him to give every man according as his work shall be, will return to that faithful servant both principal and interest" (*ibid.*, p. 660).

"Angels keep a faithful record of every man's work, and as judgment passes upon the house of God, the sentence of each is recorded by his name, and the angel is commissioned to spare not the unfaithful servants, but to cut them down at the time of slaughter. And that which was committed to their trust is taken from them. Their earthly treasure is then swept away, and they have lost all. And the crowns they might have worn, had they been faithful, are put upon the heads of those saved by the faithful servants whose means was constantly in use for God" (*ibid.,* vol. 1, p. 198).

Parable of the Sheep and Goats

And now let's shift our attention to the last story in Matthew 25, that of the sheep and the goats. At this point it introduces to us a higher level of stewardship than we have contemplated so far—the concept of helping others less fortunate than ourselves even if we receive no tax deduction for doing it. In this parable Jesus divides those in the judgment not on the basis of their belief but of their practice.

Some of us may have mistakenly thought that when Jesus returns, or during the time of the investigative judgment, He uses the list of our 27 fundamental beliefs as His standard for determining who is saved or lost. But evidently, to tell whether or not our hearts have been changed from selfish to loving, and therefore we are safe to save for eternity, all He has to do is look at our relationship to the poor.

"'When the Son of Man shall come in his glory, and all the holy angels with him, then shall he sit upon the throne of his glory: and before him shall be gathered all nations: and he shall separate them one from another' (Matthew 25:31, 32, KJV). Thus Christ on the Mount of Olives pictured to His disciples the scene of the great judgment day. And He represented its decision as turning upon one point. When the nations are gathered before Him, there will be but two classes, and their eternal destiny will be determined by what they have done or failed to do for Him in the person of the poor and the suffering" (*The Desire of Ages,* p. 637).

Of course, among the lost in His parable were professing Christians, and they did not realize that they were neglecting the one important thing that God required of them. Remember Jesus' counsel to the rich young ruler? "You still lack one thing. Sell all that you have and give it to the poor."

"Those on the left hand of Christ, those who had neglected Him in the person of the poor and the suffering, were unconscious of their guilt. Satan had blinded them; they had not perceived what they owed to their brethren. They had been self-absorbed, and cared not for other's needs" (*ibid.,* p. 639).

The Poor and the Suffering

How should we help Christ in the person of the poor and the suffering? God counsels two methods. We are first to give a consistent thank offering at church, and then also to seek out and help those in need on a personal one-to-one basis.

"In every church there should be established a treasury for the poor. Then let each member present a thank offering to God once a week or once a month, as is most convenient. This offering will express our gratitude for the gifts of health, of food, and of comfortable clothing. And according as God has blessed us with these comforts will we lay by for the poor, the suffering, and the distressed. I would call the attention of our brethren especially to this point. Remember the poor. Forgo some of your luxuries, yea, even comforts, and help those who can obtain only the most meager food and clothing. In doing for them you are doing for Jesus in the person of His saints" (*Testimonies,* vol. 5, pp. 150, 151).

"God does not mean that any of His followers should beg for bread. He has given you an abundance that you may supply those of their necessities which by industry and economy they are not able to supply. Do not wait for them to call your attention to their needs. Act as did Job. The thing that he knew not he searched out. Go on an inspection tour and learn what is needed and how it can be best supplied" (*ibid.,* p. 151).

Who are the poor that we must help? They are "His followers"— apparently the poor in the church. As Matthew puts it, "the least of these My brethren" (Matthew 25:40). The Gospel of Mark looks at the situation from the receiving perspective. "For whoever gives you a cup of water to drink in My name, because you belong to Christ, assuredly, I say to you, he will by no means lose his reward" (Mark 9:41).

The problem of poverty in a general sense could take literally all our resources and still there would be need. The church's responsibility is to help the believing industrious poor who while they practice economy still cannot supply all their own needs. The inspection tour should be among fellow believers.

"God proves us by trusting us with earthly possessions. If we are faithful to impart freely of what He has lent us, to advance His cause, God can entrust to us the immortal inheritance" (*ibid.,* vol. 1, p. 199).

God's Faithful People

The picture we receive here of how God's faithful people will live at the end of time is quite different from the practice of many today. Instead of putting a dollar into the offering plate for Sabbath school missions, they will be giving hundreds. Instead of moonlighting for additional money for themselves, they will be working extra to be able to contribute more to God's cause so as to hasten His coming. And instead of accumulating more and more, they will be divesting themselves of assets so that not much of their "stuff" will be burned up in the fires of the Advent.

"In the last extremity, before this work shall close, thousands will be cheerfully laid upon the altar. Men and women will feel it a blessed privilege to share in the work of preparing souls to stand in the great day of God, and they will give hundreds as readily as dollars are given now"

(*Counsels on Stewardship,* p. 40).

"If the love of Christ were burning in the hearts of His professed people, we would see the same spirit manifested today. Did they but realize how near is the end of all work for the salvation of souls, they would sacrifice their possessions as freely as did the members of the early church. They would work for the advancement of God's cause as earnestly as worldly men labor to acquire riches. Tact and skill would be exercised, and earnest and unselfish labor put forth to acquire means, not to hoard, but to pour into the treasury of the Lord" (*ibid.,* pp. 40, 41).

"The work of God is to become more extensive, and if His people follow His counsel, there will not be much means in their possession to be consumed in the final conflagration. All will have laid up their treasure where moth and rust cannot corrupt; and the heart will not have a cord to bind it to earth" (*Testimonies,* vol. 1, p. 197).

As we look back over our lives, most of us can distinctly remember words or phrases that made an indelible impression on our minds. Will you indulge me just a moment? I can remember as a boy the times when, following a trip my father had made to California from southern Oregon to deliver a load of lumber, we boys would shout, "Daddy's home!" That announcement made our day.

I remember when Elder Bruce Johnston, my major professor at Southern College, stopped me in the hall one day and said, "There is a conference president here today who wants to talk to you." To me that meant that someone else had recognized my call to work for God.

I remember when, following my marriage proposal, Kathy said, "Yes, I will." Then a few days later when I requested permission from her parents for the privilege of marrying their daughter, her mother said to me, "We always let our children make their own mistakes." I took that to mean that if Kathy was agreeable to the idea, they would be too.

Being admitted to the practice of law was another really memorable experience for me. Just being accepted into law school was an accomplishment. Then being a part of the 50 percent of those who actually graduated was another. But the real hurdle was to pass the bar exam and be admitted to practice. I can remember having the background check of all the schools I had ever attended, all the jobs I had worked at, all the places I had lived, etc. Then having all 10 of my fingers printed at the sheriff's office and a mug shot taken that rested on the table where I sat during the two grueling days of the exam.

At the time I finished law school only about 35 percent of law school graduates passed the bar exam on the first try. Since the exam takes place only twice a year, it is a real advantage to pass the exam as quickly as possible so you can begin your legal practice. Following the exam, you have to endure a 90-day waiting period before you receive the results. People had told me that if you passed, the board of bar examiners would send out your results in a large manila envelope with instructions on how to enter the state bar and begin practicing law. The word was that if you didn't pass, then you would get a regular No. 10 size envelope that would contain the bad news and an application to take the exam the next time.

We all knew that the results would be mailed out on a Friday. The notice would arrive in our mail on Monday, so on that day I called Kathy from the office and said, "Kat, let me pick up the mail today so that I will be the first to know the results of the bar exam." Late that morning I drove home to pick up the mail.

When I looked into the mailbox, to my shock it contained no large manila envelope. There was, however, a No. 10 size business envelope from the board of bar examiners. Only those who have been through similar circumstances can truly know how I felt at that moment. Many thoughts raced through my mind. "Why, Lord? Why me? After all this hard work and commuting, was it a waste of time and money?" My body sympathized with my emotions, and I had to sit down and calm myself. Finally after several minutes I decided that I must face the inevitable. I opened the letter, which was folded in thirds with the top down first and then the bottom folded up over the top fold. When I pulled the bottom flap down, only one sentence of the letter was visible. It said, "Good luck in your practice!" I couldn't believe it. You can imagine the trauma to my body and emotions of going from deep despair to high ecstasy in a short period of time. Then I opened the top flap and read the full letter. "Congratulations," it read, "you have passed the bar exam. Welcome to the state bar and the practice of law." The letter went on to say that under a new policy the additional materials needed would arrive later.

"Well done, good and faithful servant"

I am sure that we have all had similar experiences where we have heard special, unforgettable words. But now I am thinking of a time in the near future when all those who have taken seriously and followed God's counsel will hear those best words of all: "Well done, good and faithful servant; you were faithful. . . . Enter into the joy of your lord" (Matthew 25:21). The best I can determine is that God speaks them only to those who have been faithful in managing what God has given them. I want to hear those words more than anything else in the world. How about you?

As I look back across the pages of this book, a real conviction grips me. I now recognize that my goal as a committed Christian is to take what God has given me in time, talents, body, and finances, and bring profit to

His kingdom until He comes.

"No scheme of business or plan of life can be sound or complete that embraces only the brief years of this present life and makes no provision for the unending future" (*Education,* p. 145).

Those who prepare for eternity are at the same time making the best possible preparation for life in this world. No one can lay up treasure in heaven without finding his or her life or earth thereby enriched and ennobled. As Jesus told the disciples following His encounter with the rich young ruler, "assuredly, I say to you, there is no one who has left house or parents or brothers or wife or children, for the sake of the kingdom of God, who shall not receive many times more in this present time, and in the age to come everlasting life" (Luke 18:29, 30).

"If we use our means to God's glory here, we lay up treasure in heaven; and when earthly possessions are all gone, the faithful steward has Jesus and angels for his friends, to receive him home to everlasting habitations" (*Testimonies,* vol. 1, p. 198).

APPLICATION
Chapter 12

1. What parallels are there between the three stories of Matthew 25 and the three legitimate uses of money we learned about in earlier chapters?

2. What can or will be done to "fix" our failing economy?

3. How risky is investing in others and the cause of God, and what returns can we expect from such investments?

4. How important is helping others from the perspective of the judgment?